THIS IS LOVE

*"This is love: not that we loved God,
but that He loved us and sent His Son
as an atoning sacrifice for our sins."*

(1 John 4:10)

ROBERT GRIFFITH

GRACE AND TRUTH PUBLISHING
PO Box 338, Gunnedah NSW 2380 Australia
www.graceandtruthpublishing.com.au

All Bible quotes are from the New International Version (NIV) expect where otherwise stated.

NEW INTERNATIONAL VERSION (NIV), Copyright 1973, 1978 and 1984 by international Bible Society. Used by permission of Zondervan Publishing House. All rights reserved.

Other version quotes are from:

AMPLIFIED BIBLE (AMP), Copyright © 1954, 1958, 1962, 1964, 1965, 1987 by The Lockman Foundation. Used by permission.

ENGLISH STANDARD VERSION (ESV), Copyright © 2001 by Crossway Bibles, a division of Good News Publishers. Used by permission. All rights reserved.

NEW AMERICAN STANDARD BIBLE (NASB), Copyright © 1960, 1962, 1963, 1968, 1971, 1972, 1973, 1975, 1977, by The Lockman Foundation. Used by permission.

NEW KING JAMES VERSION (NKJV), Copyright © 1979, 1980, 1982, by Thomas Nelson Inc. Used by permission. All rights reserved.

THE MESSAGE (MSG), by Eugene Peterson, Copyright © 1993, 1994, 1995, 1996, and 2000. Used by permission of NavPress Publishing Group. All rights reserved.

REVISED STANDARD VERSION (RSV), Copyright © 1973, by Thomas Nelson Inc. Used by permission. All rights reserved.

Quotes in square brackets are the author's comment.

ISBN 978-0-6486439-7-5

TABLE OF CONTENTS

PREFACE

We live in a world where love means many things to many people. The whole concept of love is as corrupt and tainted as we are and so our search for a genuine understanding of real love is usually a futile one. It is into that quagmire of counterfeit versions of love that the Apostle John shouts the three words which begin the verse on the title page of this book: *"This is love!"* But John then proceeds to tell us what love is not. *"... not that we loved God."*

Love is never defined or discovered by looking at ourselves as the starting point. In his letter, John tells us clearly that God is love. God is the source of love, and God defines love. So love is not from us – it is from God. But John's point is even stronger than this.

We do not initiate a love for God. God initiated love toward us. God always loved first. He existed first because God has always existed and He has shown love first in a number of ways. Love that initiates is stronger than love that responds. Reciprocated love is not as great as love that was enacted without cause. Love is not that we loved God because that is a reciprocated love. Our love for God is a response, and that love is not as great as what God displays as love.

This is love: *"That God loved us and sent his Son to be the atoning sacrifice for our sins."* This is love. First and foremost that God loved us. God's love was not a responsive love because we were loving him. We were actually hating Him. We were rebelling against Him. We were disobedient to Him. But in spite of all that - God loved us!

So come with me on this journey as we discover the true origin and nature of love and learn how we can be channels of God's love to a broken and needy world.

Robert Griffith

CHAPTER ONE
Love makes the world go 'round

It has been more than sixty years since Paul Anka released his hit song, *"Love Makes the World go 'Round."* It was a great song, if you're a Paul Anka fan. So great, in fact, that there are at least ten other songs out there which are very different to each other, but all share this title. They were recorded by people like Perry Como, The Jets, The Hollies and more recently Madonna and Ashlee Simpson.

It's a catchy title and when you think of the hundreds of millions of songs, movies, poems and books which are out there about love, you could easily conclude that love does in fact make the world go 'round.

To us as disciples of Jesus Christ and members of the church which bears His name, this phrase takes on a whole new meaning. It probably should be the title of a great worship song, because love most certainly lies at the foundation of the whole Christian faith.

The gospel and the mission of Christ are all about love. That is why the most quoted verse in the Bible (John 3:16) begins with the words, *"For God so Loved the World ..."*

Of course, the Bible has a lot to say about our love and how we should show love towards God and those around us. However, our love is birthed in the love of God. That's why John wrote this foundational text, the verse upon which I will build all the chapters of this book:

> *"This is love: not that we loved God, but that he loved us and sent his Son as an atoning sacrifice for our sins."*
> *(1 John 4:10)*

Love lies at the core of who we are; why we were created and it is an intrinsic part of our nature as human beings. Love is central to the mission of Christ, the purpose of the church, the foundation of human life and the essence of our true identity.

In this book we will be exploring the foundation of the whole Christian faith and the priority of love. This teaching will affirm what many of us already know but we always need reminding and encouraging to more fully embrace who we are in Christ. It might even challenge what some you believe and that's a good thing as long as it drives you back to the Spirit of God Who is the One Who will always guide you into all truth.

This study will also give us a clear story to tell the people around us in our community. It's the greatest story ever told and when people embrace the truth of this story, they are drawn into the loving arms of God and their lives change forever. For as the Apostle Paul said in Romans 2:4, *"It is God's kindness that leads to repentance."*

I firmly believe that evangelism is the natural outflow of a healthy Church. When we truly know who we are and, more importantly, when we know Whose we are and why, then our story is really God's story and God's story will always demand people's attention and challenge them at the deepest level of their being.

But where do we start with such a huge topic as love? Well, according to Maria in The Sound of Music we 'start at the very beginning, a very good place to start.'

So, let's go all the way back to Genesis as we begin to focus on the priority and foundation of love in the Christian life, and in all life as human beings.

"The LORD God took the man and put him in the Garden of Eden to work it and take care of it. And the LORD God commanded the man, "You are free to eat from any tree in the garden; but you must not eat from the tree of the knowledge of good and evil, for when you eat of it you will surely die. The LORD God said, "It is not good for the man to be alone. I will make a helper suitable for him."
(Genesis 2:15-18)

Let me digress here and make an important observation. God created the world and He said it was good. He created a lush garden full of trees bearing fruit, full of all kinds of experiences – sensual, physical and intellectual.

He said to this new human He created (and I paraphrase here), *"You can freely eat from the lavish provision of this garden. You are to enjoy life to its fullest. But, in the very centre of the garden, in the very centre of your life, there will be a constant source of frustration for you."*

That's right, in this 'good' garden, before the fall, before sin entered the human world, God said *"Here is something right under your nose every day that you can't experience and you can't know, but will always want to."* That is to say, God built into our earthly lives from the very beginning, an element of frustration that He did not intend for us to overcome. Just let that sink in.

You see, it's not sin which accounts for all of our frustration in life. Sin is not totally responsible for all our limitations. It is not the fall of mankind that gave us all of our boundaries. God has given us some. In His good pleasure, in His sovereignty - God has limited us and assigned us frustration to some degree on some level in this life. God is the only One without limits; the only One without any frustrations; the only One Who is totally fulfilled.

So when you hear pop psychology saying to you: *'Sign up for my program and you'll be fulfilled..'* or when you hear the army recruiter say: *'Sign up and you'll be all that you can be ..'* or when you hear religion say: *'Follow these ten easy steps and you will reach your highest potential in God,'* you are being lied to. How do you know it's a lie? It's a lie because in this life, frustration, limitation and a permanent sense of 'not yet' has been designed into our human, earthly experience by God.

A lot of people end up feeling guilt and shame because of this frustration and lack of fulfilment. I have met hundreds of people like this and many are in Christian ministry. When we are frustrated; when we lack fulfilment in some area; when things aren't going as well as they could be or should be in our opinion; frustration can often develop into a personal sense of guilt or shame.

Tragically, there are many preachers and well-meaning Christian brothers and sisters out there who will fan that flame of guilt and shame by suggesting to you that your lack of fulfilment is all your fault because of your lack of faith or because of your sin or something you are doing wrong or not doing right.

Of course, a lot of our frustration will be the result of our own bad choices; some of it may well be the result of sin - ours or somebody else's - but some of our frustration is actually designed into our human life by God.

God never intended that we would be completely free from frustration. We are pilgrims on a journey and only when we reach our final eternal destination will we be completely free from this frustrating sense of 'not yet.'

I think this sense of 'not yet' and the feeling we get which tells us 'there must be more' is actually a vital part of human life and maybe even eternal life.

Therefore, if anyone promises complete fulfilment inside or outside the Church - don't believe it. The Bible doesn't promise you that. God doesn't promise you that.

In fact, God promises you a certain amount of 'not yet,' a certain amount of frustration and longing for completion in this life and He actually says this is good. He created the world that way and when He had finished, He said, *"This is good. This is the way it ought to be."*

Let's leave that important digression now and go back to Genesis 2 and see the second thing which God said.

> *"The LORD God said, "It is not good for the man to be alone. I will make a helper suitable for him." (Genesis 2:18)*

Now I know this is one of the most quoted Bible passages at weddings and I am sure that 99% of sermons ever preached on this verse talk about the marriage relationship. That's fine because these verses are certainly relevant to marriage.

However, what I want to share with you falls into the 1%. Which means I want to explore the foundational principle in this verse rather than its specific application to marriage. Of course this applies to marriage, but not only to marriage.

There is an underlying principle articulated here which applies equally to all humans, married or not: *none of us are meant to be alone.* While frustration is given to us as part of the human experience; while limitations are imposed on us; while there are some things that we long for that will not be given to us fully in this life; and that's the way it's supposed to be; there is one frustration that we are <u>not</u> supposed to endure. We are not supposed to be alone and we are not supposed to feel alone. This is one frustration that God never intended us to live with – not ever.

In fact, I would go so far as to say that the vast majority of what God has said and done throughout our whole human history is focused on ensuring that we never again have to endure the emptiness, frustration and debilitating darkness of being alone. God planned from the very beginning for us to have helpers who are 'suitable' for us, which literally means 'comparable to' us and 'compatible with' us. People whom we can love and from whom we can receive love.

Simply put, we were created to love and be loved.

I am not just talking about marriage here - not all people will be married and God is fine with that – but all people are meant to be in relationships, in community, in the family of humanity and ultimately the family of God. Nobody is meant to be alone.

Always beware when you hear someone say (and it's often to a woman who is on her own), *"Well, the Lord will be your companion and He will be everything to you that you need and desire."* At times single men cop the same line, but not as often. I'm not sure where that idea comes from - but it doesn't come from the Bible and it certainly doesn't come from God.

We just read in Genesis where God looked at a human being and effectively said: *"Even I am not enough."* According to God, we were intended to love and be loved by flesh and blood human beings. To have helpers, to have companions, to have people to be affectionate towards and from whom we can receive affection. That is part of the stuff we are made of - it's essential to our very being.

There's a longing and there's a yearning for relationship and community that God actually built into us and one which God intended would be fulfilled in us during our earthly journey.

Why is this? It actually flows from Who God is. We were created in God's image and the New Testament tells us that God is love. God is not love in the abstract. God is not love in some moral, symbolic way. God is love in His essence. God is love in relationship - because that's where love functions - in relationships. That is also the dominant theme of the entire Bible.

God the Father is the Father of somebody - that's a relationship. God the Son is the son of somebody - that's a relationship. God the Holy Spirit is the helper, comforter, and counsellor. Those are relationship terms. God is family, if you want to put it that way, and when God created us, that family circle was expanded. God the Father, Son and Holy Spirit have been in relationship or for eternity - that's essential to who God is.

And God said: " ... *let us make mankind in our image.*" In other words, "*Let's expand the family, shall we?*" Well-adjusted families often want to do that, don't they? They want to expand their circle. That desire comes from the image and the heart of God.

A well-adjusted, healthy church family doesn't want a nice little tight community for itself - it wants to expand and embrace many more brothers and sisters. That desire comes from the image and heart of God. So now that we are in relationship to God through the saving life, death and resurrection of Jesus Christ, God is not just our Creator and our Source, God is our Father.

Through the work of Jesus Christ – we now understand that God is Father to us - we are His children. God the Son is our Saviour and our shepherd but He is also our brother. God the Holy Spirit is our comforter, counsellor, advocate, interpreter and guide, but also our companion and intimate friend.

A lot of people are thrashing around looking for meaning and some kind of purpose in life, but it really is very simple. I want to suggest that for you and me and for everyone else in this world, our reason for being created, is to be people who love and are loved.

People who receive love from God and from other people and who give love to God and to other people. That, I believe, is the most important part of being human. Everything else that you do, professionally or personally, is just the foreground detail on the broad canvas of your life.

I truly believe that our primary purpose, when boiled right down, is to receive and to give love and that's why everyone can be a huge success in life regardless of age, race, gender, intellect, physical ability or status.

We are all given the opportunity to receive love and to give love to others and from my experience over the years, I can promise you that if you sincerely connect with what I am praying God will reveal to us in this book, then God can and will re-vitalise, re-new, revive, restore and re-focus your life and bring clarity, purpose and power to your ministry in the Kingdom of God.

In fact, I will go even further out on the limb here and say that a fuller Biblical understanding of love may well be the greatest need in the church of Jesus Christ. The church is in crisis across our nation and throughout the western world.

Hundreds of congregations are closing every week across the world. Countless hours have been poured into church growth conferences, books, courses, training programs, evangelism initiatives and strategies all designed to 'fix' the church.

There have been thousands of task forces, committees and councils convened to discuss the problem and the result is always the same: precious oxygen and time are consumed as we knock down another thousand trees to produce the paper on which our strategic plans and vision statements are printed and then filed in a drawer somewhere and forgotten!

Year after year after decade after decade we excel at complicating what is so incredibly simple. Love truly does make the world go 'round and a full understanding of the priority and place of love is most certainly what is needed for the church to grow and touch our nation for Christ. Let John remind us again of the source of that love:

> *"If anyone acknowledges that Jesus is the Son of God, God lives in them and they in God. And so we know and rely on the love God has for us. God is love. Whoever lives in love lives in God, and God in them. This is how love is made complete among us ... In this world we are like Jesus ... We love because he first loved us." (1 John 4:15-19)*

Jesus gave us a simple, yet profound secret to life when He told us to, *"Love the Lord your God with all your heart and with all your soul and with all your mind and love your neighbour as yourself."* (Matthew 22:37-39). Receiving love from God and returning that love to God and to those around us – it's all about relationships and for all healthy, growing relationships, you need love – God's love – which *"has been poured out into our hearts through the Holy Spirit." (Romans 5:4)*

If the Church is in crisis, it is largely because our personal relationships with God and with each other are in crisis. As we ponder what God might be saying to us and to our church today, we may like to face some probing questions: How well do we really know God, personally? How well do we truly know each other?

We share buildings, meetings, services, activities, programs and events - but do we share our hearts and lives, our fears and aspirations? Do we share love, intimacy, transparency and the kind of relationships which are the building blocks of a healthy church?

Jesus said, *"I will build my Church and the gates of hell will not prevail against it."* (Matthew 16:18). In order to do that He has to overturn the tables in our temples – in our hearts – and drive out all doubt, fear, guilt, shame and wrong theology which prevents us from entering the holy of holies – which is the very heart of God. Only there will we *"know this love that surpasses knowledge and be filled to the measure of all the fullness of God."* (Ephesians 3:19).

That's what's coming if you decide to seriously engage with what I will be sharing in this book. I truly believe Jesus is reclaiming the Church which bears His name and that means He first needs to reclaim our hearts, our worship, our devotion and our primary focus. Then, and only then, will we see Jesus truly build His church.

Let those who have ears to hear, listen to what the Spirit of God is saying to us today.

CHAPTER TWO
The Key to Life

If our primary purpose in life is to receive and to give love then everyone can be a huge success, regardless of their age, intellect, physical ability, wealth or status. The wonderful thing about the way God set things up is that you don't need to have a superior intellect; you don't need to have great beauty; you don't need to have abundant energy or extra strength; you don't really need good life chances at all. To be a complete success in life, in God's eyes; to achieve your highest purpose as a human being, created in the image of God, you just have to be somebody who has learned how to receive love and give love. Maybe you should read this paragraph again. The world is not telling you any of this!

It has often been said that life is not fair – and that's true - of course it's not fair! No one has received an equal amount of anything. If 'fairness' means everyone is the same, then life is certainly not fair. But the big equaliser is that you can be a huge success as a human being if you learn how to receive and give love. *God created us out of love - for love.* That's the main point of life.

With that foundational truth in mind, let me ask a really important question, the answer to which will determine the whole future of the Christian church (no pressure!). What is the main reason we should tell people about Jesus? What's the primary motivation for sharing our faith? Why should we share the gospel, the good news with anyone? Is it because God commanded us to do so? That may be true, but I suggest that's not the main reason to share the gospel with people. Is it because we need more people to fill our empty seats on Sunday? That may be true, but I suggest that's not the main reason to share the gospel with people.

Is it because we're afraid they're going to hell if we don't get them to wrap their minds around some foundational theological concepts? That may be true, but I suggest that's not the main reason to share the gospel with people either.

I believe the primary reason we should tell people about Jesus is because we care about them and don't want them to miss out on the whole point of life by not experiencing the love of the God in Jesus Christ! They will miss the main reason they breathe if they don't experience God's love and return that love to God and to those around them.

That's why we should want to share the good news with everyone on the planet – so they can be fully human and fully alive, as God intended; so they can experience the power, the wonder and the glory of the kingdom of heaven now as a present reality, not a distant hope beyond the grave! To miss out on receiving God's love and letting that love flow through us to others - is to miss out on the very essence of being human.

Let's look at 1 John 4:7-9 again.

> *"Dear friends, let us love one another, for love comes from God. Everyone who loves has been born of God and knows God. Whoever does not love does not know God, because God is love. This is how God showed his love among us: He sent his one and only Son into the world that we might live (i.e. have life) through him."*

To live in Christ, through Christ and for Christ is to know God's love and prove that love by being people who love. How do we know if someone really knows God? Someone who prays a lot surely knows God, right? Not necessarily. Somebody who knows the Bible really well knows God. Not necessarily.

The Pharisees knew the Scriptures better than anyone - but they didn't know God – they actually helped kill God when He showed up! Even when He was sitting down and eating dinner with them – they still didn't know God and they were experts in the Scriptures!

I am also pretty sure Satan knows the Bible inside out – but that hasn't done much for his relationship with God! Well, how about somebody who operates in the spiritual gifts - somebody who has the power of God emerging in their lives - certainly that proves that they know God? Not necessarily.

Well, what about the person who works hard for God and gives their whole life to serve God in the church - they must know God. Maybe, or maybe they just know the church. The Apostle Paul answers this beautifully in what we have called 'The love chapter.' This is my paraphrase:

> *"If I speak in the tongues of men and of angels, if I have the gift of prophecy and can fathom all mysteries and all knowledge … if I have a faith that can move mountains … if I give all I possess to the poor and surrender my body to the flames, if I do all these incredible things that we value so highly in ministry - if I do all that better than anyone else in the world - but I do it without love - then it means absolutely nothing!" (1 Corinthians 13:1-3)*

Not only that, it's a noisy gong; it's an irritation; a distraction and it adds up to zero. We don't know God and we are not participating in authentic Christianity and humanity unless our lives are characterised by love. Let's read it again:

> *"Dear friends, let us love one another, for love comes from God. Everyone who loves has been born of God and knows God. Whoever does not love does not know God, because God is love." (1 John 4:7-8)*

That's about as clear and unambiguous as you could ever get. Praise God for the piercing simplicity of His Word!

Now these insights are certainly not new – but if we take these basic truths at face value, they are quite confronting. For example, I want you to imagine how others would describe you as a person in one sentence. What would be the first, or most obvious thing they would say about you. Would people say without hesitation: *"Oh yes, she's a woman (or he's a man) first of all who loves God with all her heart, mind and soul and loves other people as she loves herself."*

As we ponder that scenario for a moment, we may be forced to conclude that most people would talk for a while about other attributes we may have before they get to the fact that we love God and other people, and we would hope they get there eventually! But maybe they would not.

That should not cause us to beat ourselves up with guilt and shame. We shouldn't lose sleep over it. We should simply thank God for His revelation and make it a matter of serious prayer, and I believe God will speak to us through this book and help us re-focus on the foundation of our faith and our lives as God's special creation.

God will continue to confront us with the priority of love because I know that the one thing I just have to get right in this life, the one thing you have to get right in this life if we are to truly be successful and fulfil our purpose is love. It truly is that important and the foundation of everything else in our lives. Visions, goals and plans are all great, but at its heart, the focus of our life - the direction in which we need to be heading if we are to be all that God created us to be and have an authentic existence is frighteningly simple:

We need to be people who are described as those who sincerely love God and love other people.

Now that's something to live for; that's something which is achievable regardless of intellect, beauty, Bible knowledge, language, culture, family history, marital status or the state of the economy. With that focus and that purpose, you don't need to take into account how messed up you were as a child or even how messed up you still are! This is something you can head towards no matter who you are and you can end up being the biggest, best and most authentic person you could possibly be and it's never too late to start. You might be 9, 29 or 89 - it doesn't matter – it's never too early or too late to learn how to love and be loved.

Of course, some of us may have some 'unlearning' to do. We may have to re-evaluate some things in our life, because there are so many people today who didn't experience a lot of love when they were growing up. There may be some people reading this right now who just never got the hang of receiving or giving love.

Love is something that you receive, but also something you learn. Love is a gift from God but it is also something you are taught. You experience love over time and then end up doing love. If you are raised that way then you learn this as a child. But sadly, many people today just didn't have that experience as a child. So, you may be one who never really got the hang of being loved and then loving others because your childhood was not the best it could be. That is sad. However, what's even sadder is that as we matured as men and women, the world around us didn't do much to change that deficiency.

For example, as an adult man, I was not told that the first thing, the most important thing I needed to do as a man, the first thing I needed to do in order to prove I had authentic manhood is to develop the capacity to love and be loved. Nobody told me that.

The world and the culture around me actually told me that love can get in the way of being an authentic Aussie male - because after all, a man accomplishes; a man achieves; a man conquers; a man dominates, a man provides. Isn't that what many of us were told by the media, our peer group and the world in general? If you can get a little affection along the way, good for you, but it certainly is not important compared to being a successful achiever and provider - in fact love can often be an obstacle to success.

What's even more amazing and sad is that when I became a Christian and eventually headed into full time ministry, I was then searching for the secret of success in the Kingdom of God. I wanted to make a difference. I wanted to change the world and as I sat in lectures in Theological College; as I read books and was mentored by Bible scholars and senior Pastors; I gained all sorts of advice and insights about how to be rooted and grounded in the fundamentals of the faith so I could have a fruitful and successful ministry.

But guess what? Not once, at least not once that I can remember - maybe I wasn't listening, not once do I remember anyone saying, *"Learn how to be loved by God first. Don't go anywhere or do anything until you learn how to receive and give love, because that is foundational to all ministry and all life, especially life in the Kingdom of God."* No one said that.

Instead, I was told I had to learn how to preach; learn how to study and teach the Bible; learn how to pray; learn how to counsel; learn how to do spiritual warfare; learn how to be a leader … and the list goes on. I was told all these things and they are all very important and could be regarded as foundational to a successful ministry also, but not once did anyone tell me that the foundation beneath all those things had to be *"the love of God shed abroad in our hearts by the Holy Spirit."* (Romans 5:5)

What I should have been told is this:

"First and foremost, before you do anything else, before you even attempt to minister in Jesus' name, learn how to receive God's love and give that love to others."

Sadly, it took many years in ministry before anyone said that to me and I can remember the time, the location, the person ... and the impact. The time: May, 1993. The location: Stanwell Tops Conference Centre in NSW, Australia. The person: Dr Ken Blue. The impact: life-changing, ministry-transforming and the beginning of the greatest spiritual battle imaginable - but that is a story for another day!

Before I wrap up this chapter, let's take a brief advance look at a passage which I hope will become our foundational reading for the remainder of this book. We have several of the Apostle Paul's prayers recorded in Scripture - this is one of them.

> *"For this reason I kneel before the Father, from whom his whole family in heaven and on earth derives its name. I pray that out of his glorious riches he may strengthen you with power through his Spirit in your inner being, so that Christ may dwell in your hearts through faith.*
>
> *And I pray that you, being rooted and established in love, (because you are rooted and grounded in love – you then) may have the power, together with all the saints, to grasp how wide and long and high and deep is the love of Christ, and to know this love that surpasses knowledge - that you may be filled to the measure of all the fullness of God."*
> *(Ephesians 3:14-19)*

When you got out of bed this morning, I wonder if you realised that you, little old you, can actually be filled to the measure of all the fullness of God Himself?

You can be everything a human being was created to be (inside those limitations in Genesis 2 that I mentioned); you can achieve your purpose as a man or woman or young person if you are rooted and established (or grounded) in love, because God is love and if you truly know God then you will experience and express God – you will truly love.

In this book I am praying that God will show us again what that means and what that looks like and the Holy Spirit is going to change lives and re-arrange priorities and replace wrong ideas and wonky theology in our minds as we explore what it truly means to have the very roots of our lives deep in love (deep in God); as we explore what being grounded in love actually means for us today.

In these first two chapters, I just wanted to set the scene for what I believe God will unwrap for us and reveal to our hearts and minds in the remainder of this book.

CHAPTER THREE
Rock Solid Foundations

Some years ago, a ministry colleague of mine told me a story about a builder he knew when he lived in Canada and this story serves as a great illustration of our lives. This builder was constructing a large, luxurious two-storey house which overlooked a golf course. It was towards the end of winter and the temperature had been well below freezing for many weeks. The builders over there are accustomed to the cold weather and this builder couldn't afford any down time so his team put on their woollen beanies and their working gloves and pushed on through the freezing temperatures.

Now in that part of the world, to build such a house they usually dig this massive hole which they can finish into a liveable basement if they like or just keep as a storage area. But beneath that hole they drill down and construct some reinforced concrete piers deep enough below the ground to find some bedrock. Then they pour the reinforced concrete floor and walls to form the basement and the foundation for the two levels of house above. They put centre pier supports on top of the basement floor and then pour a reinforced suspended concrete sub-floor on top. Only then, when that strong foundation is complete, can they commence building the main house which everyone will see.

So, this builder and his team laid the foundations as they had done so many times before. Then they began building this very impressive house. After a couple of months, they were running ahead of schedule and were now constructing the roof. The weather was warmer too. The gloves and beanies were off and the whole team were up on the roof in the glorious spring sunshine nailing down the last sheets of plywood, upon which the shingles would be laid.

Then it happened ... everything changed in the blink of an eye! As they had all climbed to the top of the house and began to work that morning, something happened which had never happened before to this builder or his team in their whole careers and it was frightening, to say the least. As the combined weight of these four tradesmen shifted to one side of the roof, the entire house lurched forward and off to one side.

Just imagine it. You're on top of this huge two storey house, working away, when in a matter of seconds, the whole structure decides to become the next Leaning Tower of Pisa! The crew went flying, ladders toppled over, tools fell to the floor below or the ground and the builder himself just laid there on the piece of plywood he had been nailing. As he looked around at his now broken masterpiece, this astute builder said, *"Something is wrong here."* As he clung to the only rafter left exposed, this discerning tradesman thought: *"I doubt this is what the owners had in mind when they contracted me to build their dream home. This house has got to be fixed. But first of all, I need to find out what the real problem is here."*

He proceeded to pull up one of the pieces of plywood and carefully dropped down to the top floor. He looked up and saw that every rafter was now twisted - some of them were actually splintered and broken. He said, *"Well, that's got to be fixed - but that's not the problem."* He went to his wonderful spiral staircase connecting the two floors and noticed it had totally torn away from the top floor. He said, *"Well that's obviously got to be fixed - but that's not the problem."* Then he shimmied over and hung and let himself down onto the ground floor and he looked at the windows on the east side and they had all popped out of their frames and one of them had shattered in the process and the door jamb was now a parallelogram instead of a rectangle. Once again, he said, *"That's got to be fixed - but that's not the problem."*

He then went into the kitchen and opened the now twisted door that led down into the basement. He grabbed his torch and sat down on the stairs and looked into the basement. He shone his torch towards the eastern corner of the house, which was now the lowest point of this tilted, twisted mess. There he saw this massive crack in the concrete slab at the very base of the whole structure. That's when he finally said, *"Now that's the problem and that is where we have to start."*

They had laid the concrete foundation for this massive house in sub-zero temperatures which is not a problem – as long as you leave considerably more time than normal for the concrete to cure. Even though concrete generates its own heat - it needs a lot more time in cold temperatures to cure properly.

So, the builder now concluded that he must have started building too soon and the concrete eventually cracked and gave way under the weight of the building. But it still didn't make sense to him. Such an extreme amount of movement and damage should not have occurred from a cracked slab. So, he would need to go even deeper.

His suspicions were confirmed a week later after they had demolished the whole house and excavated underneath the basement. The concrete slab was not even the real problem. The underlying cause of this disaster was much deeper and completely invisible. It was actually the piers beneath the foundation which were the problem. One of the piers below the bottom slab was not resting on bedrock, but clay.

They simply had not drilled down far enough on the east side. The bedrock was another three feet below and some lazy tradesman had stopped short when he thought he had hit rock. Perhaps he believed the design of the house with its massive all concrete basement was more than enough support.

Therefore, when he hit some pretty hard clay, he decided to pour the concrete pier on that side and the clay turned out to be soft after some rain, combined with the weight of a concrete basement and a two-storey house. The moral of this story? *It doesn't matter how great your building is, a weak foundation will eventually bring it down.*

They had to demolish absolutely everything and start again, this time with a rock-solid foundation. The second house they built looked exactly like the first one, but the difference was massive, you just couldn't see it. The strength, stability and long-term viability of that home was now very high, because it had a strong, supported foundation which would now last a lifetime.

That story basically sums up this chapter and maybe even this whole book! Many people experience what that house did at some point in their life. Just as it took months of building before the weight of the house was sufficient to challenge the weakness in the foundation, so too it can take years of living before our foundations are challenged and found wanting.

When that happens - the result is just as devastating as the above story, as our outwardly strong house; our carefully constructed life, starts to tumble. At such a time, we need our qualified Master Builder, Jesus, to take us on a tour down through the various levels of our life until we find our foundational problem.

Now from my experience over many years, having been called in as a 'building consultant' as people's lives lurch to one side and threaten to collapse entirely, I have found that in the vast majority of cases the foundational flaw in all of those people's lives is most often the same. The bedrock beneath every secure, stable, strong, enduring Christian life, must be God's love.

The starting point, the foundation beneath this complex and magnificent life we have spent years constructing, must be God and God is love. The unconditional, never-ending love of God has to be our point of reference; the cornerstone; the bedrock we drill down to and upon which we build the piers, the basement, the floor, the walls and the entire reality of our life.

Christian counsellors will testify to this. A good counsellor is like a building inspector inspecting the construction site of a house that is about to collapse or has already collapsed. As they talk with the person, they will discover various symptomatic problems.

For example, the person might struggle with depression, anger, fear or resentment and there are ways of coping with each of those things - but none of those issues are the real problem. So, like a building inspector, a good counsellor moves further down to the heart of the building. On the way they may discover all kinds of fears, doubts, destructive habits and many things which need to be fixed for the person to be healthy again. But those things are not the main problem, they are merely the symptoms or the by-products of a deeper problem.

The real problem always lies at the foundation level and for many of us, those emotional, relational, psychological and theological foundations were never laid properly or cured correctly and so we have not grounded our house on the bedrock of the revelation of God's love in Christ. It may take years but eventually our 'house' will begin to fall.

I believe this modern parable of a poorly constructed house applies to every single one of us, regardless of how loved we may have been as a child, because every one of us was born into a sinful, fallen, broken world.

As such, we were born with a huge flaw in our foundation already. That flaw is called sin and from the very beginning, sin created a strong barrier to us fully experiencing God's love personally and intimately. We may have been blessed to have God's love flowing through our parents and others but many people didn't even have that. Even if we did, in our sinful condition we were all born outside of the full experience of God's love.

Now God has always loved us. He loves His whole creation. But we were cut off from knowing or experiencing God's love personally from the day we were born until that barrier of sin is removed in our minds and our hearts. That is exactly what God did in and through Jesus Christ. That's why they call the Gospel good news! Praise the Lord! God sent His own precious Son to take your sin and mine upon Himself so that anyone who embraces His free gift of love and salvation will discover that the barrier to God's love has been removed by the life, death and resurrection of Jesus. As that revelation comes, our spirit is regenerated and we are born again into a new relationship of love and intimacy with God. The entire foundation of our life is effectively replaced at that moment.

Jesus, the man, may have been a carpenter but, Jesus the Christ was the Master Builder (Creator) Himself in human flesh and He came to totally re-create, rebuild, renew and re-construct the very foundation of our lives. So now from God's point of view there is no longer any barrier; no longer any obstacle to His overwhelming love flooding into our lives and transforming us from the foundation of our being and impacting every part of our life.

For God so loved the world, that He gave His only Son. God gave His Son for the world - that is, every last human being ever to have lived.

The barrier between every single human being and God's love has been removed, once and for all time - in Christ, through Christ and for Christ!

Therefore, if there is no longer any barrier, from God's perspective to His life-changing, nation-transforming love flooding our very being and flowing through us into the community around us; if our sin no longer separates us from God, because all sin has been atoned for by Christ and in Christ, then we need to face some hard questions:

> Why are there just as many believers seeing counsellors and therapists as there are unbelievers?

> Why are there just as many Christian marriages ending in divorce as non-Christian marriages?

> Why is the joy of the Lord not oozing out of all believers and inspiring all those around them?

> Why can we pack 80,000 screaming, excited, joyful fans into a football stadium to watch a bunch of grown men play with a piece of leather for 80 mins, while at the same time, the people of God, the ones who are supposed to know the secret of life and are supposedly filled with the fullness of God Himself, gather in decreasing numbers in funny looking buildings to meet with their like-minded brethren to worship and encounter this God, and most of them leave the same way they arrived: no happier, no more empowered or transformed or impacted in any significant way?

What have we missed? There can be only one answer and we won't like it. Many of the people sitting in church buildings this week are yet to fully understand and fully encounter the awesome power of God's unconditional, overwhelming, life-changing outrageous love!

The incomprehensible love of God has not fully penetrated our experience in a tangible, observable, foundational way. The full reality of what God has already done in eternity for us through Christ has not burst forth into the experience of so many people in churches right across this nation. That dynamic, powerful, heart-wrenching truth of God's love and grace still needs to make that 40cm journey from our heads to our hearts.

Perhaps we've known this love that surpasses knowledge, but we may have allowed the pressures of life in this world to rob us of that experience as we lost our first love. Millions of Christians across the world have spent years, maybe even decades, building this great big house - their life. They have worked hard to become successful as a husband or wife or father or mother; as a businessperson or employee; as a disciple in the Church. They have built this enormous, impressive, outwardly beautiful house - their life - but deep down, below the floor, below the basement even, in that hidden place, there is a flaw in the foundation of their life, in their thoughts or their theology or their understanding of themselves, their God and the world - or all of the above!

The most serious flaw and the most common foundational deficiency is the same for many: they never really learned how to receive the fullness of God's overwhelming love – from which flows His amazing grace, His abundant mercy and His cleansing forgiveness. It is entirely possible for us to be heavily involved in the life of the Church all our lives and still not fully embrace the radical fullness of the Gospel.

This can happen to any of us. In our head we understand the love of God; we can read about it, talk about it, sing songs about it, write songs about it, be moved by it, teach it, even share it and lead people to Christ - but none of that means we are really experiencing the fullness of the love.

Knowledge of God's love does not guarantee we are living day by day in the power of God's love - truly experiencing God's love, knowing God's love, letting God's love bomb-proof our life as we grasp how central, how permeating, how foundational God's love is to every part of humanity. That is not the experience of many Christians.

Perhaps you are relating to this right now and you know without a doubt that I'm talking about you - that's great - keep engaging with this teaching because God has a treat for you which is far beyond your wildest imagination! Or perhaps you are one who is thinking you do know God's love experientially - and if that's really true then your life will be showing that in so many ways and you will be saying 'amen' to all this and you will be really encouraged because the Holy Spirit will be affirming God's truth in your experience. That's great - be affirmed and then pass this teaching on to others.

But there will also be those who think they know God's love but have actually settled for second best or third best and are yet to really taste the sweetness and depth of God's love and experience the transforming power of this love which is truly out of this world!

Regardless of where you are on that spectrum, I plead with you to persevere and press on with what I am going to share in this book. I would encourage to take time after each chapter and let it percolate within you as God prepares you to venture further into what I believe could be life-changing teaching for many. I am not going to do anything amazing; I am just going to read some Scriptures which we've had in our possession all our lives, tell some stories and expound some clear truths of the Gospel. I am just a messenger who has been called by God to be faithful to the message He has given me.

I sincerely believe God is going to do a lot in and through those who embrace the message I bring here. I have faith that God is going to refresh, renew and revive many of His people as He confronts the barriers to His love and pours out His very essence and presence into our lives and into His Church like never before.

Regardless of where we are now in our pilgrimage, we can all grow into a person who has been overwhelmed by the love of God and who knows how to receive that love and, in the process, the Holy Spirit is going to renew the very foundation of our lives. With that solid foundation of God's love - there is no danger of our house ever moving off its foundations again.

And friends that is what I want for all of you. That is what God wants for all of us and that is why I am praying for you what the Apostle Paul prayed for his brothers and sisters in the Church in Ephesus all those years ago:

> *"For this reason I kneel before the Father, from whom his whole family in heaven and on earth derives its name. I pray that out of his glorious riches he may strengthen you with power through his Spirit in your inner being, so that Christ may dwell in your hearts through faith.*
>
> *And I pray that you, being rooted and established in love, (because you are rooted and grounded in love – you then) may have the power, together with all the saints, to grasp how wide and long and high and deep is the love of Christ, and to know this love that surpasses knowledge - that you may be filled to the measure of all the fullness of God."*
> *(Ephesians 3:14-19)*

Are you hearing what God saying here? Do you believe that it's possible for you to be filled to the measure of all the fullness of God?

I know it is mind-blowing. It is incredible. It is beyond our comprehension. But it also happens to be God's plan and purpose for you and for me and the whole reason we live and breathe. It's also God's plan and purpose for all those people who are not with us yet – those who are not part of the life of the Church yet. What better time to connect them with the liberating good news - the love of God - the gospel of Jesus Christ? Don't be selfish and keep all the blessings for yourself - spread them around! When you finish this book, give it someone the Lord has laid on your heart and ask them to read it. Then pray for them every day, that God will draw them to Himself.

God is speaking to us all at this critical time in the life of the church. A fresh wind of the Holy Spirit is blowing across God's people. The Spirit of God has been working behind the scenes for many years, preparing hearts, positioning people, releasing gifts and laying the foundation for a whole new chapter in our journey as the church.

I plead with you to open your mind, open your hears, cultivate a teachable spirit, and I promise you, God will bring you a revelation of Himself and His plan and purpose which is beyond your wildest imagination, because we belong to a God Who is able to do exceedingly, abundantly more than all we ask or even imagine, according to His power that is at work within us. Do you believe that?

We belong to the God Who has promised He will bring to completion that which He began in each of us. We belong to the God in Whom there is no condemnation for those who are in Christ Jesus because through Christ Jesus, the law of the Spirit who gives life has set us free from sin, from guilt, from shame, from every barrier and obstacle and doubt and fear which can hold us back from being right in the middle of the next great move of God in our nation.

This teaching is not just for us. We are not here to just be reminded of the great truths of the gospel – as important as that is for us all. We are here to be equipped to take that gospel to those who are not with us on this journey yet. As our lives are transformed by the power of the God's love; as we are filled to the measure of all the fullness of God, that love will overflow and people around us will notice. When you are full of God – everyone notices! They may not know it's God in you that sets you apart in this broken and dysfunctional world, but they will be drawn to His presence and they will want to know more.

The future of the church and the mission of Christ in our community and our nation is in our hands as God's people. We are not called to build the church, we are called to testify to the life-transforming love of God in Christ Jesus to any and all those whom God leads our way. As we fulfil that calling, Jesus can and will build His Church in us and through us.

Lord, we believe ... now help us in our unbelief! Come, Holy Spirit, come, renew our heart, firm up our foundations, overwhelm us with Your Love, revive Your Church, Lord. Amen.

CHAPTER FOUR

Christ in Us

I have a ministry colleague in the United States, who has nine children, all of whom were home schooled by his wife, and back at the beginning of this amazing challenge, both parents made a commitment to God and to each other that their highest priority was to teach their children how to read and how to love and be loved - then they would be a success in everything they do. These parents firmly believed that these two things would give their children the educational, emotional and spiritual foundation on which they could build any life they chose.

Now of course they were taught many other things but teaching them to read and develop a love for reading and teaching them to receive love and to give love, undergirded everything this amazing mother said and did as she shaped her nine children and prepared them for life. That was many years ago now and all of those nine children have moved into their adult years and they all love the Lord and are all actively involved in the mission of Christ. Last time I checked, two of them were serving in overseas mission work; most of them have university degrees, at least one has a master's degree and is studying for his Doctorate. But above and beyond all that, each of these children have learned how to receive and give love and that is by far the most important foundation we can lay in every life, especially the lives of our children and grandchildren.

As I have explored this whole area of love over the years, I have gained a much clearer picture of what the church of Jesus Christ can and should be and, even more than that, I have seen what the church which Jesus is building really looks like and is becoming right now.

When people embrace the gift of God's grace in Christ and are brought into the life of the church, I don't want any of them to ever hear, *"Well, now that you're a Christian, here's a list of important things that you need to do."*

For hundreds of thousands of believers entering the church, the very first message they hear after *"Welcome to Church,"* was often something like:

> *"Well now that you're in the Church, you have to learn how to read the Bible; you have to learn how to pray and witness and tithe; you have to show up to all the meetings; you have to stop swearing; you have stop smoking; you have to stop hanging around with those friends who don't share your Christian values ... etc."*

Maybe they weren't told they 'had to' do these things, but the unspoken message was clear that these are the spiritual disciplines they 'should' embrace if they wanted to be a faithful Christian who pleases God.

I've seen the lists. Some of them are printed on the back of the very gospel tracts that are used to lead people to Christ and the message is clear: *"Welcome to Church - now here's a list of behaviours, disciplines and service we (and God) expect of you as a disciple of Christ and a member of the Church."*

Many of us have been told that salvation is a free gift from God, but sanctification is our job and it requires discipline, sacrifice and a lot of hard work. God gets us through the gate, free in Christ, but we have to take it from there!

The term 'sanctification' means 'growing and maturing in Christ'. Some preachers teach that it's what 'working out our salvation with fear and trembling' means.

Now this concept of salvation and sanctification somehow being separate - one being solely the work of God and the other being primarily our responsibility through discipline, sacrifice and hard work – is still widely taught and accepted in the Church even though it cannot be found anywhere in the New Testament! When you study the New Testament and examine the original Greek and look at the theological principles outlined there, you will not find a single verse to support one of the most widely held views about living the Christian life.

I remember being told and reading in reputable Christian journals and books, that my salvation and my sanctification are totally separate activities. One is God's job and the other is my job, in partnership with Holy Spirit. *'Grace gets you into the Kingdom of God, then through spiritual disciplines and hard work, we advance the Kingdom and please God.'*

 I was given that verse in James which says faith without works is dead, and that was always interpreted as an imperative for me to add good works to my faith so my faith would be effective, alive and real.

Many years later, I studied the Greek in that same passage in the book of James and discovered it effectively says the exact opposite of how many people interpret it. What that passage in James really means is simple: *If your faith is genuine, if your faith is in God (not in faith itself) then the good works will follow as the fruit of the life that is within you.*

The good works, spiritual disciplines and the activities and ministries we commit to in the life of the church should be an outflow of the love and presence of God in our lives. Otherwise, they are nothing but dead religious works. It really is that simple.

Now please understand what I'm saying here (and not saying): There is absolutely nothing wrong with all the spiritual disciplines. The question is: what is the source, the power, the motivation and the focus which lies beneath those disciplines? We can get things horribly wrong when we get this wrong and that can be very damaging to us as disciples and equally damaging to the ministry of the whole church.

There is actually only one thing that a new believer really should do first and foremost and it's exactly the same thing I would exhort mature believers to do also, and that is to become rooted and grounded in God's love. That's the first and the highest priority - before anything else comes. We need to take whatever time is necessary to establish that deep foundation in our lives by word and deed and wait for it to set. Then we can build whatever we want on that foundation of God's love.

If I had any vision for the church, it would be this: I would like the church to not be known primarily for its preacher and his sermons; I would like the Church not to be known primarily for its ministries and the things we do in serving others; I would like the Church not to be known primarily for its great worship. My hope, my desire and my prayer every day is that we become a people who really know and experience the love of God; a people who are filled to the measure of all the fullness of God, Who is love. Then, and only then, can that love, God's love, flow through us into the lives of those around us in our church and in our whole community and nation.

Until we minister and serve out of the fullness of God's love; the reservoir of God's love, we do so in our own strength and all that will amount to is more burned-out believers and a rapidly shrinking church.

When Jesus walked among us all those years ago, He was asked one day what the most important commandment is, and He bounced right back with those all too familiar words: *"Love the Lord your God with all your heart, soul and mind and love your neighbour as yourself."* Now please, I beg you, don't race off after this chapter and beat yourself up, trying harder to be better at loving God and loving people.

Don't come away from this chapter thinking, *"Robert hit the nail on the head. I really need to get better at giving and receiving love."* In Jesus' name, please don't even think that way! It is that kind of works-based religious thinking that has bound up millions of sincere, well-intentioned Christians across the world in a spirit of religion!

There is only one way to get good at loving God and loving people - only one way - and that is to first receive and bask in the love of God. God is love and God is radiating His love to us constantly, but unless we open ourselves up to God and other people as vehicles of God's love, we will never truly experience His love in the way He intended. We must receive God's love before we can be channels of God's love and that is a daily reality.

You and I are fallen, sinful, rebellious and broken humans. We have nothing to offer God, nothing to offer the church and nothing to offer the world. We are empty, until God fills us with His presence and power. That's why John told us in his first letter: *"This is love, not that we love God but that He first loved us."* (1 John 4:10).

So, if you want a really simple goal for life and a priority for our Church for the days ahead, how does this sound:

Rediscover God's love and then be filled to the measure of all the fullness of God, Who is love.

Then, and only then, out of that abundance, out of that overflow of God's incompressible love, can we be a blessing to others in whatever ministries we feel equipped for and passionate about at this point in our journey.

Do you remember the WWJD movement in the 1990's? It began in America and spread throughout the world. People were wearing these WWJD bracelets everywhere. WWJD stands for *'What would Jesus do?'* and the intention was that the constant reminder of this question in our daily lives was supposed to help us ponder what Jesus would do in any particular situation. This then was a prompt for us to go and do likewise. That sounds like a pretty good way to live, right? Well, millions of WWJD bracelets later, the church is weaker and less effective than ever.

What went wrong? Did we simply lack the commitment and courage to act, once we worked out what Jesus would do if He were here? Or perhaps we may have been asking the wrong question and that entire movement was flawed theologically from the beginning.

If, as the WWJD marketing campaign suggested, we think that we should pause at every key decision point in our lives and try to imagine what the Jesus of the gospels would do if He were here now and then imitate that, then that is a load of theological bunkum which will only produce powerless, frustrated, ineffective believers who inadvertently bring themselves and all those they influence back under old covenant law.

Let me explain it this way. Who am I? I need to start there first. I am an English-speaking, Australian Christian; born in the twentieth century, living in the 21st Century. I am married, with five children and ten grandchildren; I live in a modern, technologically advanced western society.

Now by contrast, the Jesus of the gospels was an Aramaic speaking Jew, born in the first century; He was never married; had no children or grandchildren; He lived in a relatively primitive ancient culture and He was many years younger than I am now when He got himself killed. Now the only way those two humans could be more different or more disconnected from each other is if one of us was a female! In human terms, we have nothing in common.

Now I am sure that if Jesus the man showed up today in Australia and not in the Middle East in the first century, then we may have something to work with here and if He did, I can guarantee the Gospels would then be written very differently. But He didn't. So, I cannot begin to imagine what someone born over 2,000 years ago in a completely different culture, a different society, a different religious environment, might do if He was stuck in peak hour traffic in Sydney at 5pm - because Sydney didn't exist in Jesus' day, nor did cars, nor did airplanes, nor did the crazy lifestyle and culture and worldview of today.

It's like me trying to imagine what my great, great, great, great, great, great, great, great grandfather would do if he were here today sitting at my computer, looking at the internet. That's a nonsense question!

Now you may be thinking, that's not what people mean here. They are not asking what would Jesus the man do in this situation, they are talking about Jesus the Christ. WWJD is not, *"What would Jesus the carpenter do?"* It is supposed to mean, *"What would Jesus the Messiah do?"* Ok. point taken, but does that make it better? Does that make any more sense? No! It makes it worse because it's a load of theological nonsense. Asking, *'What would Jesus do if He were here?'* suggests that Jesus isn't already here and it suggests that Jesus has not already done everything.

In the Kingdom of heaven, where we live and move and have our being in Christ, through Christ and for Christ, the reality is that every single situation you and I will face has already been dealt with by Jesus! Every challenge you face in your life has already been overcome by Christ and in Christ. Every problem which may present itself today or tomorrow in your life has already been solved by Christ and in Christ and He is present now and active in our lives through His Spirit to bring the fruit of His finished work into our lives. **We are not called to imitate Jesus; we are called to surrender to Jesus.**

Therefore, perhaps it's time we started a new movement and manufactured some new bracelets with the acronym WHJD: *What Has Jesus Done?* The answer to that question will be: *everything!* Your salvation; your entrance into the Kingdom of God; your sanctification; your growth and maturity in your faith; your spiritual gifts and passion for ministry; your fruitfulness and joy in ministry; your faith; your courage; your healing; your wisdom and the clear revelation of God Himself … it has ALL been secured for you already, in Christ, through Christ and for Christ.

When Jesus hung on that cross and said, *"It is finished,"* He really meant it is **finished**. God's reconciling work is now complete, from God's perspective and in God's kingdom. You and I and all mankind are now invited to believe, receive and walk in that reality. Believe the truth that Jesus has done it all for us and receive the fullness of God's love and grace and presence and power.

Then, and only then, out of that abundance, out of that overwhelming experience of the love and grace and the presence of God, will flow faith, prayer, a passion for the Bible, a heart for people, a commitment to serve; your giving will increase in all areas of your life.

Your lifestyle and values will become more conformed to Christ in you, the hope of glory ... and all of that will be the fruit of what you have received from God, Who is love. None of that will be religious duty or well-intentioned good works done in the flesh. It will be the fruit of the Life that is within you, the Love that has been lavished upon you.

Every imaginable spiritual discipline will emerge in your life without you straining, groaning or flogging yourself with guilt and shame. It will simply emerge as the fruit of God's presence in your life, the natural and automatic outworking of God's love deep within you.

Have you ever walked through an orchard when the fruit is forming on the trees? I grew up in Orange (named after Prince William of Orange, not the fruit!). Orange is located on the central tablelands of NSW and when I was a child our city was surrounded by orchards. Cherries and apples were our primary crops. For decades we had the annual 'Cherry Blossom Festival' and the main street would be closed with people lined up five deep down both sides to watch dozens of floats and displays parade past for an hour; some bright young girl would be crowned 'Cherry Blossom Queen' and there was a market day, a town hall concert and a huge ball.

As the years passed, we produced more apples than cherries and the festival stopped and Orange adopted the name: *The Apple City.*

So, I have been in a lot of orchards and there is this amazing miracle which happens in an orchard as the fruit is forming. When the trees are very young, they are just trees, with wonderful leaves and a beautiful shape and they certainly look great all in rows across a whole orchard. But they are just time-consuming, money-swallowing ornaments taking up space - until the day arrives when the fruit starts to form.

What a miracle that is and when you are there, standing in the middle of that orchard watching that abundant, rich, succulent fruit appear before your eyes from nowhere, guess what you can hear – if you go right up close to one of those trees? Guess what you can hear? Absolutely nothing! Isn't that a miracle? There's no grunting, no groaning and no straining on the part of the tree. The fruit just forms. If the tree is well fed and watered, the fruit will always form and it will always be rich and succulent. If the tree is healthy it doesn't have to exert any extra effort to produce the fruit. It just forms automatically because that's the God-ordained purpose for that tree.

Hello? Are you getting this? Are you still with me? Just as a healthy, well fed and watered tree in an orchard will always produce rich, succulent fruit, so too will a healthy, well fed and watered disciple of Jesus Christ always produce rich, succulent fruit in their life and within the life of the church. Trees don't have to 'do more or try harder' or discipline themselves or beat themselves into submission to bear fruit. Trees just need to be still and know that the fruit is already within them – just as their Creator intended. If they are healthy, the fruit will always appear, in season – that is guaranteed.

If we are not producing rich, abundant fruit as trees planted in God's orchard, God's kingdom, it can only be because we are not healthy trees receiving the right nourishment; we are not being fed the correct food. What is our food? Jesus told us a very long time ago and His words are recorded in John's gospel.

> *(Jesus said) "Do not work for food that spoils, but for food that endures to eternal life, which the Son of Man will give you. For on him God the Father has placed his seal of approval."*

Then they asked him, "What must we do to do the works God requires?"

Jesus answered, "The work of God is this: to believe in the one he has sent."

So they asked him, "What sign then will you give that we may see it and believe you? What will you do? Our ancestors ate the manna in the wilderness; as it is written: 'He gave them bread from heaven to eat.'"

Jesus said to them, "Very truly I tell you, it is not Moses who has given you the bread from heaven, but it is my Father who gives you the true bread from heaven. For the bread of God is the bread that comes down from heaven and gives life to the world."

"Sir," they said, "always give us this bread."

Then Jesus declared, "I am the bread of life. Whoever comes to me will never go hungry, and whoever believes in me will never be thirsty." (John 6:27-35)

What is our water? Listen to Jesus' words to the Samaritan woman at the well all those years ago:

"Everyone who drinks this water will be thirsty again, but whoever drinks the water I give them will never thirst. Indeed, the water I give them will become in them a spring of water welling up to eternal life." (John 4:13-14)

The source of our food and drink is Christ in us. It is the gift of God's Son, our Lord and Saviour and His indwelling presence and love within us, which is the source of all life, all power, all gifts, all effectiveness and all fruit in the Kingdom of Heaven. We don't need to imitate Jesus or strive to be like Jesus – we simply need to surrender and let the Spirit of God transform us into the image of our Lord and Saviour.

CHAPTER FIVE
Opening the Door to Love

In an earlier chapter I shared a story about a beautiful home which was being constructed on a faulty foundation. As the structure of the home grew during the building process, the weight finally challenged the weak foundations and it gave way - resulting in a major disaster. I then suggested that the foundation of our lives can be flawed in the same way if we have not really learned how to receive love and give love.

Another analogy I think is helpful is that of a circulatory system. If there is a 'bloodstream' to our emotional and spiritual life – then it has to be love. Love is what flows between us and God. Love is also what circulates between us and others around us.

Now you can do all kinds of great things in Christian your life - you can pray; you can read your Bible; you can volunteer in some community service, you can serve the Church in some leadership role; you can bless people with acts of kindness - you can do whatever you desire to do; but love should be at the core of all those things. Every legitimate ministry should be motivated and empowered by love and the source of that love must always be God.

Now of course if there's something faulty in your blood, your whole body suffers. You may get by for a while but if you put enough stress on your body then a faulty blood supply will eventually bring your whole body down. So too with our spiritual life. If we don't truly understand the love of God or have never really learned how to receive the fullness of God's incredible love, then sooner or later the weight of our life and the pressures upon us will challenge that core deficiency and our whole life, in spiritual terms at least, will be in real trouble.

Unfortunately, this truth can be so subtly disguised and even deliberately hidden by Satan. The enemy of God loves to see us build impressive, outwardly magnificent lives. He convinces us that who we are on the outside is what life is all about. He does not want us to examine our foundations or what is at the core of our being.

If that strong foundation of God's love has not been firmly established; if the life's blood of God's love is not flowing into us and then through us, then eventually we will see all kinds of problems emerging in our lives. They might be physical problems, emotional and relational struggles; anger or jealousy; lust or destructive attitudes; performance orientation can take over which may give rise to compulsive work habits; a spirit of criticism; marriage problems and the most common one of all – depression and anxiety. When our emotional and spiritual foundation is not strong, so much can go wrong.

The ability to receive the love of God deep into our lives and allow that love to fill us to overflowing so it then touches those around us, is foundational in every respect in our lives. This is true first of all in a chronological sense. As a newborn baby you needed to be loved in a way that you understood. When babies cry, they need to be taken care of. They need to be loved by having their needs attended to. They need to know that we are coming when they cry.

This is a foundational experience for every human being. From the first day we open our eyes we need to know that there's love in the world. We can't know the philosophical aspects of love - we just need to know that somebody's there to take care of us - that's love. That is the bedrock layer of the foundation of love. If that is laid securely then a lot of other skills or abilities to receive and to give love can be built on top of that.

Now it is also true that the ability to receive love and to pass on love is foundational not just psychologically - but it's also foundational from a theological point of view. We have already read Ephesians 3:14-19 more than once in this book and that is because it contains the essence of this whole teaching. Let's take another look.

> *"For this reason, [Paul says] I kneel before the Father, from whom his whole family in heaven and on earth derives its name ... [Remember God is big on 'family'] ... I pray that out of his glorious riches he may strengthen you with power through his Spirit in your inner being, so that Christ may dwell in your hearts through faith. And I pray that you, being rooted and established in love, may have power ... [then, having a foundation in love, then you will be able] ... together with all the saints, to grasp how wide and long and high and deep is the love of Christ, and to know this love that surpasses knowledge - that you may be filled to the measure of all the fullness of God." (Ephesians 3:14-19)*

God's desire and plan for us is that we would experience life in abundance. If that is to happen - then what is wrong with us needs to be healed and what doesn't belong needs to be removed so that more of God's personality, more of God's wisdom, more of God's being, more of God's power, more of God's essence, which is love, can invade our lives.

That's what it means to be *"... filled to the measure of all the fullness of God."* That's where we are headed. That's the promise of God to each one of us here now: that we will be filled to the measure of all God's fullness!

God is love and so to be filled to the measure of all the fullness of God is to be filled with, saturated with, overflowing in love. But Paul reminds us that this will not happen unless we are rooted and grounded or established in love.

Now a lot of western Christianity has taught, either directly or by inference, that we need to be rooted and grounded in our performance. Despite what the Bible says about being rooted and grounded in love, the church has been guilty of teaching sloppy theology and legalism, so we end up believing that what we do for God and for others is what's most important in our Christian faith.

When I became a Christian, I soon learned all the things that I had to do to be a good Christian: I had to pray; I had to read the Bible; I had to tithe; I had to attend church services and activities; I had to serve in some ministry. All these are good things to do but all too often we can be given the impression that the quality of our Christian life depends on our effort and our performance. Nothing could be further from the truth! If we believe that lie then we are heading in the wrong direction as soon as we leave the starting gate! Eventually, years later, we wake up to find our whole life has shifted on that flawed foundation and it is about to collapse, and we wonder what went wrong. Quite simply, what went wrong is we didn't hear the true Gospel of Jesus Christ, we didn't receive the truth about ourselves and God from the start.

Please notice I said that we didn't hear the truth of the Gospel – that doesn't mean it was not preached - we may have just chosen to hear something else. Why is that? Why do we fall for the lies of religion? Perhaps it's because that's what the whole world around us teaches and so we are trapped into thinking that the church is like the world. Sadly, it often is, but it shouldn't be.

We can so easily get caught up in this deceitful humanistic philosophy - it's all around us. For example, the foundation of your education is the marks you are given which reflect the quality of your effort.

The foundation of your earning ability is the quality of your hard work - your ability to make the right choices - your ability to meet the right people. There is no doubt that the quality of your life in worldly terms depends primarily on your performance and your actions.

Now in the kingdom of God, your efforts are certainly not worthless - they are very important, but I'm talking here about the foundation which lies beneath your efforts. If you take nothing else from this book, remember this:

In the kingdom of God, the quality of your life depends not on what you do for God or others, but on believing and receiving what God has done for you and continues to do for you, in you and through you - in Christ.

That's the first priority and until we are secure in that, until that foundation is laid firmly in place, we should forget about all the things we want to do for God. We have to let God do it for us first and I'm not talking about a once-off reality here at the beginning of our journey. This is a daily reality throughout our entire life. Receiving from God first, before giving to God and others.

I can clearly remember the day God turned the lights on for me and I embraced His saving grace for the first time. I was 14 years old and it was a Friday night after a BBQ run by the Churches of Christ youth leaders in my hometown. I had grown up in the Presbyterian Church but had never really 'owned' my parent's faith. But I did that night. I was overwhelmed by God's grace and love for me and I can remember how real His presence was on that cold winter's night when our youth leader prayed over me. It was an amazing time indeed and yet within weeks I jumped onto that good old performance-based, 'let-me-pay-God-back-for-His-grace' treadmill and I was off and running!

I was leading a junior youth group within a month. I was a lay preacher and lay presider before I was even 16. Now God blessed those kids I was leading in spite of me. I just opened the door and let them in each week and He did the rest. God also used me as a young preacher and presider at the Lord's Supper, but my foundations were still very weak. God hadn't even put His initials in the concrete before I started rapidly building my own house!

I look back now and I really wish I had just sat in church services, listened to the sermons, studied the Bible and had people pray with me until that foundation of God's love was firmly set. I really wish I had done that for the first year or two of my Kingdom journey. It would have been so much better if I had just been allowed to get used to God holding me and loving me like the new spiritual baby I was. But instead, I built my house in record time and it was a huge house indeed. Quite impressive, so I thought!

Of course, if you want a life that's abundant and fruitful and world-changing, then by all means get involved in church, give generously, invest your life in ministry, pray for the sick, feed the hungry, release the oppressed. Do all those things and more - but just make sure they are the fruit of something far deeper and more important; make sure all that service and discipline and good works are flowing out of the reservoir of God's love in you. Make sure they are the fruit and don't try to bypass the tree itself - your relationship with God.

Otherwise, you will be caught in the trap of performance-based religion which is an abomination before God and it will only burn you out and toss you aside one day because none of us have the stamina to 'perform' for God for any length of time. We all run out of motivation, inspiration and determination.

Learning to receive the love of God - being filled to the measure of all the fullness of God - and then seeing that fullness - that love - overflow from your life into the lives of others and back to God - that is what an authentic, fruitful, effective Christian life looks like.

> *"This is love: not that we loved God, but that he loved us and sent his Son as an atoning sacrifice for our sins."* (1 John 4:10)

God's love must be the foundation of our lives. But His love must also permeate every room of that grand 'house' we build upon that foundation of love. When God comes to us at our conversion and at various times throughout our life - He invades our house, as it were. He enters various rooms in our life by His Holy Spirit. When He enters - He enters as love because God is love - and when His love enters the various rooms of our heart and soul and memory, His love heals and cleanses and restores and fixes what is wrong with us, because that's what love does. The more that God presses deeply into who we are; the more God permeates and saturates our being, then the more His love will affect us as we are healed, restored and empowered.

One of the many issues in our life which God deals with is fear - His love casts out fear.

> *"So, we know and rely on the love God has for us. God is love. Whoever lives in love lives in God, and God in him. In this way, love is made complete among us so that we will have confidence on the day of judgment, because in this world we are like Jesus ..."*

What he's saying here is that as love is perfected in us - we become like Jesus. That's why we can be bold and confident on the day of judgement because there's no fear in us.

We can be bold because we have been filled to the measure of all the fullness of God, Who is love!

> *"...There is no fear in love. But perfect love drives out fear because fear has to do with punishment. The one who fears is not made perfect in love. We love because He first loved us."* (1 John 4:16-19)

We can see John going in this circular way. We love because God first loved us and the effect of that love is that we then love. The effect of love is that it casts out all fear and when all fear has been cast out, we know that we have been perfected in love.

Fear and phobias are large and painful problems in the Christian community today. Fear in whatever form it comes to us is crippling and humiliating. Let me clarify what I mean by fear in this context. I am not referring to what the Old Testament talks about as the 'fear of the Lord.' That is a Godly, reverent, worshipful 'fear' and it refers to an awe, a holy respect before God.

The fear I am talking about here and in our next chapter is what we would normally refer to in our day as fear: an unhealthy caution, anxiety, stress, being afraid, scared, debilitated or intimidated by someone or some event or circumstance in our life. Now that kind of fear is anything but Godly and it can often be found lurking in the shadows in one or more rooms in the impressive 'house' we build – our life.

I really believe that through this teaching the Holy Spirit wants to get into those rooms and cast out that fear and even more so, He will give us the wisdom to minister to those we might know and love who suffer from this debilitating fear and don't even know it.

God wants to shine His light into those rooms - those memories - those experiences which Satan is using to hold us back and cripple us in our Christian walk and by so doing, cripple entire churches in their ministry. The Holy Spirit wants to fill those rooms with the love and presence of God, thereby casting out any fear that may still be there. He wants to get into the nooks and crannies of our life, the rooms that have been closed to Him, He wants to flood those dark places with His love and banish any and all fear.

You might wonder why He hasn't done that already. The reason is simple. The doorhandles to those rooms are on the inside. We have to let the Spirit of God in. Those 'rooms' which harbour debilitating memories and so many negative emotions are often shut from the inside. That well known verse in Revelation 3:20 says, *"Behold, I stand at the door and knock. If anyone hears my voice and opens the door, I will come in and eat with him, and he with me."* That verse is so often used in reference to conversion. We are given the picture of Christ knocking on the door of the unbeliever's heart - begging to come in and save him or her. It is featured in so many evangelistic rallies. It may even have been the verse you responded to when you came forward one day or made a commitment to the Lord.

However, if we want to be true to the context of that famous verse, we should never use it in that way because this verse is actually addressed to believers – to Christian disciples already following Jesus - and I believe it refers to what I have been saying here. As believers, we need to open the door of every room in our life and let Jesus come in and fill them with the light, love the presence of God.

I'm reminded of the Pastor who knocked on the door of one of his Parishioners, to see how she was going after some recent illness, and there was no answer.

He listened for a moment and heard something inside and realised she was home, so he knocked again. Still no answer. He took out his business card and smiled as he wrote on the back of it: 'Revelation 3:20.' He slipped it under her front door. When the lady found the card she went to her Bible and read these words: "*Behold, I stand at the door and knock. If anyone hears my voice and opens the door, I will come in ..*"

The following Sunday as the people were leaving church, the same woman slipped a little white card into the Pastor's jacket pocket as she left. The Pastor was not the only one with a sense of humour. When the Pastor got home, he looked at her card it just read: 'Genesis 3:10.' So he opened his Bible to read this: "*I heard you in the garden, and I was afraid because I was naked; so I hid.*"

Brothers and sisters, hopefully that funny story will forever remind you that God is knocking on those doors in your life today and every day and perhaps the lives of those we love and care about, but often we feel naked and ashamed and we too hide from Him and the only reason we would do that is because we have not been rooted and grounded in His love.

If we do let Him in, He will give us a spring-cleaning like never before as His love removes all trace of fear, doubt and anxiety. But He only comes in where He is invited and our fear and ignorance can keep those doors closed to the love of God.

God is always doing some spring cleaning, some healing, some restoration and redecorating in some people's lives and I believe He has more to do in the days ahead and I would encourage you to stay connected with this teaching and be prepared for Him to do some amazing things as His love fills all the rooms in your life, especially those ones whose doors may have been shut tight for a long time.

We need to trust God. He made us. He knows how we work best. He knows that the only way we will experience the abundance of life in Christ this side of glory, is if we allow His love to saturate every aspect of our lives. We can trust Him to be gentle with us. God only enters those rooms in our life as love, for God is love, He cannot enter any other way and we will never be the same when He does, because God's love is always transformational.

You simply cannot encounter the love of God and remain the same because His plan and purpose is to transform you and me and all people on this earth into the image of His Son, our Lord Jesus Christ and He does that by the power of His love. When that happens, we will stand in awe once again in the face of a love so amazing, so divine, it truly will demand our soul, our life, and our all.

All we need to do right now is come to Him, just as we are. Religion tells us to clean up our lives before we stand in the presence of God. Religion tells us we are blessed and loved when we obey and serve and perform for God. Jesus tells us the truth. Jesus bids us to come, just as we are, every day, and let Him love us back to life.

So come to Him now . . trust Him with your heart . . trust Him with your secrets which are no secret to Him . . let God overwhelm you with love – unconditional, unending love. Bask in that love, let it do its work in you and you will be surprised by what happens in your life. Wounds will heal; doubts and fears will depart; courage and trust will grow as you rest in the loving arms of your Lord and Saviour Jesus.

This will not only be a blessing to you, but it will also bless all those around you. When you are overwhelmed by God's love, your judgement of others disappears.

When you truly understand that you are who you are all because of God, not because of anything you have done, then you will not look down your nose at others.

You will realise that it's God's kindness that leads to repentance (Romans 2:4) and not the judgement of others. Let God's love overflow into all your relationships and watch what His Spirit will do in the lives of those for whom you are praying to come to God and never, ever forget the truth John gave us:

> *"This is love: not that we loved God, but that he loved us*
> *and sent his Son as an atoning sacrifice for our sins."*
> *(1 John 4:10)*

CHAPTER SIX
What has God Done for Us?

If you can, I want to ask you to read this next statement out loud – at least a couple of times. I shared it in the last chapter but it is too important to only read once!

In the kingdom of God, the quality of my life depends firstly not on what I do for God or for others, but on what God has already done for me, and continues to do for me, in me and through me.

In light of that truth, I want to ask and answer a question today: *'what has God done for us?'* We would need many hours to answer that fully, but Paul's words in Ephesians 1:3-14, which I regard as some of the most profound in the entire Bible, are a great place to start. I'm reminded of the words in that famous poem by Elizabeth Barrett Browning, *'How Do I Love Thee? Let Me Count the Ways.'* I guess my question today is, *'How does God love us?'* and the Apostle Paul will count the ways - as I provide just a little commentary in between his profound statements. So, are you ready for a mega-dose of grace and truth? I hope so. Let's begin at verse 3 of Ephesians 1.

> *"Blessed be the God and Father of our Lord Jesus Christ, who has blessed us in Christ ..."*

God loves us in a myriad of ways. However, the pinnacle of His love; the magnitude of His love; the depth of His love is revealed fully and overwhelmingly in Jesus Christ – in the spotless life, sacrificial death and glorious resurrection of Jesus Christ – in Whom we are raised to new life also. *'In Christ'* is Paul's most repeated phrase in all his letters and for good reason.

"(God) has blessed us in Christ with every spiritual blessing in the heavenly places …"

Notice the past tense leading into this amazing promise. It says that God <u>has</u> blessed us with every spiritual blessing in the heavenly places. It's a done deal. This is not just a promise of what is to come. The only reason we may not have experienced every spiritual blessing in the heavenly places yet is because we have not fully embraced the power and reality of *"Your Kingdom come, Your will be done on earth as it is in heaven."* The more we pray that prayer and press into God and believe His Word, then the more we will experience what God has already given us in Christ:

"… just as He chose us …"

Here we read three of the most defining words of our entire Christian life. God chose us. Therefore, if we say, *"I made a decision for Christ,"* or *"I accepted Christ,"* or *"I asked Christ into my life,"* those statements distort the true gospel and reveal an ignorance of the very foundation of our faith and the Christian life, which is: *God chose us.* Whatever it is we did, or do now, day by day, can only ever be a response to God choosing us. Why did God choose us? The answer, quite simply, is love – outrageous, incomprehensible love. This Love, this God, chose us:

"… in Christ before the foundation of the world …"

Not only did God choose us, but He chose us before the foundation of the world. God didn't choose me in 1973 when a youth leader prayed over me and I embraced Christ as my Saviour for the first time. My salvation was already a reality long before Adam was created. Then one cold night in 1973 the Spirit of God opened my eyes to that truth and I began to walk in that reality and my life has never been the same since.

God chose us before we had a chance to do anything to mess it up. Let me say that again: God chose us before we had a chance to do anything to mess it up and He chose us ...

"... *to be holy and blameless before Him* ..."

Really? Is that what it really says? When we look into the mirror we scratch our heads, because what we see in there is neither holy nor blameless. That's because we are looking in the wrong place. Do you remember what Paul's favourite phrase was? *'in Christ.'* This wonderful salvation is ours is *in Christ.* We are already holy and blameless *in Christ* – we have to be - otherwise we are wasting our time praying and trying to enter into the holy presence of God in worship. Unholy vessels cannot be in the presence of a holy God, they will be burned up in the purity of His holiness. So, we pray to God - *in Christ.* We worship God - *in Christ.* We are holy and blameless before God - *in Christ.* Then, just in case we are too thick to work it out for ourselves, Paul tells us that all of this is done by God...

"... *in love.*"

This is love – not that we loved God but that He loved us. This is God. God is love. Then Paul shows us what this love, this God is really like, when he says:

"He destined us for adoption as His sons and daughters ..."

We are not just His disciples, not just His subjects or His servants; and we are certainly not His pawns on some great celestial chess board - we are God's adopted children - and like all adopted kids, we are loved with an extra special love ... and that was all made possible ...

"... *through Jesus Christ, according to the good pleasure of His will* ..."

Do you know that God actually takes pleasure in you? He enjoys you as any parent enjoys their children. Sometimes I think we refuse to accept that God takes pleasure in us because we focus on us and our sin, not on God and His love. God's calling, saving, redeeming and reconciling work in Christ is all according to His good pleasure, and it is …

"… to the praise of His glorious grace …"

It all comes by His grace: our loving restoration, renewal, salvation and sanctification is all by God's grace alone. None of us deserve to even breathe, let alone enjoy the company of a Holy God as His adopted, much-loved children! It all comes by God's grace …

"… that He freely bestowed on us …"

Let me ask you something. How much does something cost that's free? Nothing? Are you sure? Are you really sure? When I observe the behaviour of we Christians across the centuries and still today with so many of us, I could be forgiven for thinking that we have to pay for the greatest free gift known to mankind. That's what religion tells us and I beg you in Jesus' name to never use the word *religion* again to describe anything to do with the Church Jesus is building! God hates religion! Religion gives you rules, requirements, expectations and obligations on behalf of God. But our God, the One and only true God, only gives freely and unconditionally. Is it any wonder that God hates religion with a passion?

That's why Jesus castigated the Pharisees of His day for creating qualifying criteria for the people of God. They added law after law which needed to be obeyed in order to please God and earn His favour and enjoy His blessing. That's a lie!

We cannot buy God's grace or love or blessing or gifts or power or presence with our obedience or our service or our attempt at living a holy life or by giving more money or time or passion or whatever currency we choose to use. God has nothing for sale! (And if He did, we could never afford it anyway!) God will only give to us freely, unconditionally and without obligation. We are never 'much obliged' in our relationship with God. That very concept is an offense to His free grace and love.

We don't gather as the church each week because we are 'obliged' to. We don't worship because we are 'obliged' to worship. We don't give because we are 'obliged' to give. We don't follow God's Word and plan for humanity because we are 'obliged' to. We don't pray out of 'obligation.' We do all those things and more because we freely choose to - in the freedom God has given us in Christ. If you do feel 'obliged' to be part of the church then perhaps you should go and do something you really want to do and choose to do, because God is not interested in your obligation. He only wants your free love response - to His free love and grace. Any other response to Him is religion - not a love relationship - and God hates religion!

Now if you want a religion there are plenty out there to choose from - just don't let Satan turn what God has done in Christ into a religion, where we slap a loving, gracious God in the face by doing things for Him out of obligation. Freely, freely we have received, and freely, freely we will give ... or we won't. Everything comes from God freely ...

"... in the Beloved. In Him we have redemption ..."

Notice it doesn't say 'we will have redemption.' Nor does it say, 'we are working our way towards redemption.' Nor does it say, 'we long for or hope for redemption.'

It says, 'In Him (Christ) we <u>have</u> redemption.' How?

"… through His blood …"

The pardon for all our sins, past, present and future - has already been signed by God the Father with a pen dipped in the blood of His own Son. That is why the cross stands at the centre of our whole Christian faith because without the death of Christ, there can be no redemption, there can be no salvation, there is no eternity in the presence of God … and in this redemption through His blood we have …

"… the forgiveness of our sins …"

We <u>have</u> forgiveness. It doesn't say 'will have' or 'may have if we confess the right way.' We already <u>have</u> forgiveness of our sins, past present and future, before they were even committed - in fact, before we were even born. If I asked you the question, *"When were you saved?"* How would you respond? I bet many of you would think of a particular day or an event in your life. But theologically speaking you would be wrong. Millions of Christians refer to the day in their life when they were saved and the assumption is that they were not saved before that day. That's not what the Bible teaches.

Your personal experience of your salvation may have a starting point in your earthly journey. Mine was in 1973. There may well have been a point on your historic timeline when you personally embraced the gift of your salvation and it became real. But theologically speaking, biblically speaking, God saved you from the consequence of all sin before you even knew what sin was, before you were even born, in fact. Even more shocking and amazing than that: God saved you from sin before the foundation of the earth, in the eternal, timeless Kingdom of heaven.

Now of course, the physical reality of the atonement - the life, death and resurrection of Jesus - broke into time and space in this earthly kingdom at a particular point in our history over 2,000 years ago and we bear witness to that event every time we write the date. However, that was not the beginning of our salvation. So it's wrong for me to say, *"My salvation began in 1973."* It's just as wrong for me to say, *"My salvation began when Jesus died and rose again."* If that's true, then what about Abraham, Moses, Ruth and all God's servants before Christ's death? They're in big trouble if salvation was secured thousands of years after they died! No, the only accurate statement any of us can make and be true to God's Word and not cast all the people of God before the cross out into the cold, is to simply say that we were saved before the foundation of the world, in the heart of God …

> *"… according to the riches of His grace that He lavished on us."*

It's God's grace from the beginning - you don't get in any other way – and it's God's grace every day – you don't get along any other way. God made sure there was nothing of us in our salvation that we could doubt it later on or take pride in something we did to secure it. God wanted the foundation of our faith and our relationship with Him to be 100% secure and that means we cannot be part of securing that at all – because we are fallen, broken people who get it wrong more than we get it right and nothing we do can ever be trustworthy enough to last a lifetime, much less for eternity.

Because of God's love for you, He made sure your eternal security in Him, your eternal salvation, redemption and reconciliation was totally and completely secure, which is why He effected your salvation before He even created you.

The rest of the story from then on is just the glorious and wonderful detail in the picture. That's why Paul, in his exuberance and overwhelming sense of God's love, says that God lavished His grace upon us.

It was like he was trying to find the most qualitative and quantitative adjective to describe this love, this grace, this God. He lavished this grace on us. And yes, there's even more …

> *"With all wisdom and insight He has made known to us the mystery of His will …"*

In this amazing salvation, this mind-blowing, wonderful, eternal relationship God has secured for us in Christ, we are given a just a glimpse into the mystery of God's will. This revelation has come in and through Christ in these last days to you and me and all believers in Christ.

What a blessing it is to be born on this side of the cross where the manifold wisdom, plan and purposes of God is now fully revealed to us and through us to the rest of God's children who don't know that's who they are, yet! And all of this is …

> *"… according to His good pleasure that He set forth in Christ, as a plan for the fullness of time."*

What you and I get to live out in this time and place is all part of God's master plan from the very beginning. We may not understand it, but by faith, we embrace the assurance that God is in control and He knows the end from the beginning. Paul says here that God plans …

> *"… to gather up all things in Him, things in heaven and things on earth. In Christ we have also obtained an inheritance …"*

Notice again the past tense. Our inheritance is already ours, in Christ. The complete manifestation and experience of that inheritance; the unfolding wonder of all that is ours in Christ is a life-long adventure of discovery. But we don't strive to achieve it, we simply believe it and receive it. Now there's a religion-busting slogan for your fridge door: **Don't strive to achieve it, just believe it and receive it!**

We have obtained this inheritance …

> "… having been destined according to the purpose of Him who accomplishes all things according to His counsel and will …"

In the midst of our broken and mixed-up lives, here is our rock, our foundation and anchor point: God will accomplish all things according to His counsel and will. If we walk only by sight and develop our theology from what we see around us or in the mirror or on the evening news, then we will end up with a confusing, impotent, powerless God. But if we learn the lesson of Abraham and believe God in spite of the circumstances which surround us, then amazing things will happen in our head, in our hearts, through our lives and in and through the church so that we, who were the first to set our hope on Christ, might live for the praise of His glory.

> "… In Him you also, when you had heard the word of truth, the gospel of your salvation, and had believed in Him, were marked with the seal of the promised Holy Spirit."

Have you ever read and understood anything in the Bible? Have you ever prayed and seen God answer your prayer, no matter how insignificant you thought it was? Have you ever discerned the hand of God at work in the world, in your family or in your Church?

Have you ever felt the presence of God in a hymn or song or prayer or during a worship time? If you answered yes to any of those questions, then I have some really great news: you have been marked with the seal of the promised Holy Spirit and you don't ever have to doubt the presence of God in your life again.

You see, none of those things can be humanly discerned or understood. Only the Holy Spirit can interpret Scripture to your spirit; minister the presence of God to you and open your eyes to see and discern the things of God. You don't need some 'higher' blessing from God, you just need to believe the truth of God's Word which says, as a believer, in Christ, you have been marked with the promised seal – the Holy Spirit of God and ...

> "... this is the pledge of our inheritance towards
> redemption as God's own people ..."

This is a down-payment, a deposit, a taste of things to come. Whilst we live in two kingdoms, the temporal kingdom of this earth and the eternal Kingdom of heaven, we will experience the fullness of the presence of God in increasing measure over time. As we press into the heart of God and experience in our lives more and more of what He has already given us completely in Christ, all of this will be ...

> "... to the praise of His glory." (Ephesians 1:3-14)

Wow! What a passage and I have only just scratched the surface in my commentary here. We could devote a sermon to each verse, each phrase, each word in some cases!

So, with all that truth behind us, let's read this statement out loud once more:

In the kingdom of God, the quality of my life depends firstly not on what I do for God or for others, but on what God has already done for me, and continues to do for me, in me and through me.

And what has God done for you? According to the passage we just explored from Ephesians: everything! Everything you could ever imagine, plus some!

Welcome to the Good News! Welcome to the Gospel! This is why our life in Christ is anything but religion! At the heart of religion, you will find a list of things you have to do to honour and please God. At the heart of the Christian faith, you will find Christ, Who has already done everything that religion expects you to do. He has achieved everything that legalism says is your job – and He has given that to you as a free gift, once and for all time by His grace!

Jesus Christ did what no human had ever done before - He fully obeyed the perfect law of God. He scored all 'A's on his heavenly report card as a man and then He did the most amazing, outrageous thing imaginable: He paid the price for our inability to obey the law of God – He suffered and died on our behalf.

Then he conquered sin, death and Satan once and for all time as He rose from the dead and ascended to the right hand of God the Father. But then ... please get this ... then, Jesus approached the throne of God and handed His report card to God which now has your name and my name on it, and He declared, *"Father, it is finished."*

This is love. This is God - a God Who has loved us with a love so deep and wide and high and strong that we could explore its riches for ten thousand years and still only be skirting around the edges!

Before I finish this chapter, I want to ask a favour of you. What you have just read is far too important to just say 'amen' and move on. I really encourage you to take a break and pray about what you have read here and perhaps even take the time to read this chapter again before moving on. The riches of God's Truth in this one chapter and in that one passage from Ephesians are enough to satisfy your spiritual appetite for years to come. If you want to make sure the foundation of your faith is rock solid and will never shift or move, then this chapter is one you should re-visit often.

I also want to issue you with a challenge for this next week. You are free to accept this challenge or not, nobody but you and God will know anyway! I want to invite you to read Ephesians 1:3-14 every morning, for a whole week, before you embrace the challenges of each day - and preferably out loud. Then every night before you go to sleep, I want you to read Psalm 23.

Then in my next chapter I will talk about fear which is the greatest barrier to embracing God's incomprehensible love personally. We will ask God to deal with whatever fear is left after the Holy Spirit has used Paul's words and David's words to remind us of some important truths and challenge any underlying unbelief we may have which is the seedbed of all fear.

So come, Holy Spirit, speak to us and reveal Christ to us and in us. Amen.

CHAPTER SEVEN

Fear Not

In the previous chapter we took a closer look at the Apostle Paul's amazing words in Ephesians 1:3-14. This passage contains some foundational truths which impact everything we think about God, His love and our relationship with Him and those around us. The Apostle John also gives us some powerful words in the fourth chapter of his first letter when he simply states that: *God is Love.* So, at the very core of Who God is, you will find love and at the core of what true love is, you will find God.

Therefore, when God comes to us, He always comes to us in love. This is so important for us to grasp. It's that simple and that clear. But I'd suggest there are millions of sincere believers today in the worldwide church who have not yet fully embraced this foundational truth. They may affirm God's love in their minds, but in practice, many Christians still feel accused or judged and like they don't measure up.

We can read the Bible verses which proclaim our salvation and our freedom in Christ; we can sing the victory songs together on Sundays; we can proclaim and preach God's forgiveness, grace, mercy and love, but still live like it's all about our performance; we can still feel like we just don't make the grade. So where does all that condemnation and guilt come from?

Well, in the first instance, it comes from our failure to hear or accept the true gospel of God's saving grace, but in the spiritual realm the Bible tells us that all accusation against God's much-loved, forgiven children comes from 'the accuser' - Satan. If you ever feel accused in your spiritual walk, it is never God who accuses you.

It is always the lies of the accuser aided by your tortured conscience which prevent God's love and grace from being fully effective in your life. But that accuser has no authority in God's kingdom and the law of God against which he accuses us has already been fulfilled completely by Christ, and we now stand in Christ, in His perfect performance before the Holy law of God. Satan still accuses, that's his job – we simply need to ignore those accusations. Jesus has overcome the accuser once and for all time:

> "Then I heard a loud voice in heaven say: "Now have come the salvation and the power and the kingdom of our God, and the authority of his Messiah. For the accuser of our brothers and sisters, who accuses them before our God, day and night, has been hurled down." (Revelation 12:10)

Because of the finished work of Christ, there is no longer any basis upon which the devil can accuse us. Jesus fulfilled the law of God and gave that fulfilment to us as a free gift. So now we stand in Christ: in His perfect life; in His atoning death; in His powerful resurrection; in His victory over sin and death and Satan - once and for all. That's where you and I live and move and have our being (Acts 17:28). That's our reality before God. We are *in Christ* and this all comes to us in love:

> "This is love: not that we loved God, but that he loved us and sent his Son as an atoning sacrifice for our sins."
> (1 John 4:10)

Now when we allow this outrageous love, this outrageous grace, this outrageous God, full access to our heart, our mind, our schedule, our imagination; when we give God access to all the 'rooms' in our spiritual, emotional and relational 'house,' then amazing things happen!

The first and most important thing this God, Who is love, does, is drive out fear, because, as John tells us:

> *"There is no fear in love ... perfect love drives out fear ..."*
> *(1 John 4:18)*

So what fear am I talking about here? Well, some fears we will be conscious of, but many of them we probably don't even know are there and yet they can control our actions, our inaction, our faith and the degree of freedom which we enjoy in Christ.

So let me give you a 'top ten' list of fears which from my experience, are the most common fears that consciously or sub-consciously lurk in the hearts and minds of believers. Some people are victims of all these fears, some only have one or two that come against them, but any one of these can rob us of the experience of being filled to the measure of all the fullness of God. So, in no particular order, here are the top ten fears:

1. Fear of not being saved or losing my salvation
2. Fear of the unknown
3. Fear of punishment from God
4. Fear of failure
5. Fear of being outside of God's will
6. Fear of people (being hurt again)
7. Fear of Satan (demons - spiritual warfare etc.)
8. Fear of the supernatural (miracles, gifts etc.)
9. Fear of losing control
10. Fear of death

Now I am sure there are many other fears which impact us in our journey, but if we could overcome these top ten, then I think we would see millions of people set free in their walk with God and the church would explode with joy, hope and spiritual power!

Just think about this for a moment. Imagine how your life would change if you were 100% assured of your salvation and equally sure that nothing you can do or fail to do will ever jeopardise your eternal security in Christ?

How would your life be changed if you were completely assured that God's punishment for sin, all sin, all your sin, past, present and future, has actually been dealt with by Jesus and God will never punish you – not ever?

How would your life be changed if you no longer worried about failure? What risks would you take? What adventures would you embark upon? What bold steps would you take for God and for others if you thought that as far as God was concerned, you can never fail – only learn and grow?

How would your attitude to life change; how would your prayers change; how would your life be transformed if you stopped trying to work out what God's specific will was for your life, your family or your Church? Can you even imagine how many millions of prayers seeking God's will on a myriad of issues would cease in an instant if we were to discover God's will for us? Can your mind comprehend how the church would be transformed and empowered when the fear of being 'outside' God's will was driven out forever? Could that happen? Of course it could.

How would your life change if you no longer let past hurts, grief or the memory of people's actions towards you hold you back from trusting people again, believing in people again, opening up to people again, being vulnerable again? So many people who are disappointed or hurt by others, withdraw more each time until they end up with a wall around them which nobody can penetrate – not even God. How awesome would it be if that wall was completely destroyed forever?

How would your life and your church be transformed if you knew that Satan, the most powerful created being in the universe, the archenemy of God, the tormentor of the saints, the accuser of the brethren - has actually been defeated? If you no longer had to wait until the end of your life on earth for the power of the evil one to be rendered void in your life; if you could actually live a life which was substantially free from the attacks of the enemy? Can you even imagine the freedom, the courage, the confidence and the abundance you would then enjoy as a believer in Christ?

What if God were to reveal to you that His supernatural power, gifts and miracle-working grace were never meant to be confined to Jesus and the original Apostles, nor are they the exclusive possession of what we have wrongly called the 'Pentecostal' arm of the Church?

What if you were to discover that the same power which raised Jesus from the dead was actually flowing into you as a believer, 24 hours a day, 7 days a week and that power can flow through you to those around you anytime you decide to believe it and embrace God's empowering presence in your life?

What if you were to really accept that there is only one Lord, one faith, one hope, one baptism, one Holy Spirit working in all and through all and that all the gifts of the Spirit and all the fruit of the Spirit are actually in Christ and you are also now in Christ? Wow! Maybe that's why Jesus said the truth will set you free! Perhaps that is why they call this the gospel – the *good news!*

How would your life change if you were no longer afraid of losing control; if you no longer needed to understand everything about God before stepping out; if you no longer feared things you have not experienced before?

What if pressing into the heart of God and seeing His Kingdom plan and purpose fulfilled through your life, your church and your community became far more important to you than your reputation, your image, your appearance or your composure? Can you imagine what God could do with that level of trust and submission?

What about the biggest fear of all – death? You might say you don't fear death, until it stares you in the face and then your heart is revealed. But how would your life change if you not only didn't fear dying at the end of a long and fruitful life, for we all die someday; what would life be like if you didn't fear death at any time – even tomorrow?

Can you imagine what the church would look like, sound like and act like if nobody feared death, no matter how old or young we are? Perhaps it would look like the church in the book of Acts. Perhaps it would look like the church Jesus promised to build. Perhaps it would look like the church was always supposed to look like.

Well, I'm not sure any of us have an imagination that big - to ponder how we and the church would be if all these fears could be removed, now – right now - and the reason we don't ponder that scenario is because we don't believe that such a possibility exists this side of the grave. Did you hear those simple, but confronting words? I hope so, because this is the key to this whole chapter; it's the key this whole book; it's the key to our abundant life in Christ; it's the key to absolutely everything in the Kingdom of God.

These three simple words explain why all these fears (and hundreds more) will continue to haunt us and hold us back: *We don't believe.* Now I don't want to minimise the very real issues people struggle with in their lives.

I don't want to demean the work of counsellors or therapists or mentors or anyone who, in Jesus' name, are sitting with people day after day trying to help them overcome their fears and the things which hold them back in life. That is not my intention. Nor was it Jesus' intention to personally attack or ridicule the well-meaning spiritual leaders of His day when He called them white-washed tombs and a brood of vipers when they failed to set God's children free by the truth! Like Jesus, I just want to proclaim the truth - God's truth – no matter how uncomfortable that makes people.

Simply put, there's one underlying issue which provides the fertile soil for all those fears to germinate, grow and flourish as they squeeze the very life out of us, sometimes literally. I am referring to the sin of *unbelief*. We simply don't believe God. We don't take Him at His word and live according to what He has already revealed to us and secured for us in Christ.

It really is simple: if you fear, then you don't believe God - you don't fully trust God. In the final analysis, the sin of unbelief is the cause of all the fears I have just mentioned. Every week there are millions of dollars and millions of hours spent in therapy and counselling across the world by people who are trying to break free from the things which rob them of the life God intended them to have. I can save them all that money and time right here and now and say, *"Just believe God! Just believe what God has said and done already."* Many years ago, I probably would have criticised someone for being so simplistic and reducing something so complicated and personal to a basic statement like, *"Just believe God."* But after decades of ministry among God's people and decades of seeking the heart of God myself, I realise that we Christians have become experts in taking what is profoundly simple and then complicating it beyond recognition!

Why do we do that? I believe it's because we don't like the simple answer! There is a legalistic, religious inclination in our fallen nature which refuses to accept that the Christian life could ever be that simple. *"Just believe God!"* That is a statement which gets right up our religious noses, just like Jesus' words in Matthew 11:30 got up the religious leaders' noses when He said, *"Take my yoke upon you … for my yoke is easy, and my burden is light."* I could take you into any Christian bookshop tomorrow and point you to fifty books which will try to convince you that living as God intended in this hostile world is the hardest thing imaginable. But in Christ, living an abundant, powerful, effective life, free from fear and anxiety, is not only possible, it is guaranteed.

Have you wondered why throughout the Old Testament, we hear God saying through His prophets the same thing over and over and over and over and over and over again? *"Do not be anxious"* … *"Do not fear"* … *"Do not be afraid."* In the New Testament we see the same appeals from Jesus and Paul and the other Apostles to not fear and not be anxious. Why are there so many exhortations from God to not fear and not be anxious? The first reason is because that's what fallen humans are inclined to do all the time. We are anxious and fearful by nature and that nature is fallen, corrupted, fallible and sinful. We were not created to be anxious or fearful which is why God has continually pleaded with us to not fear.

However, we can miss the second and most liberating fact about all these appeals from God to us to not be anxious or fearful about anything. They are not just commands; they are actually promises from a loving Father! Do you think God would ask us to do something that was not possible? Would this loving God, Who gave His only Son to secure our salvation, actually exhort us to be something which we cannot be? How cruel would that be?

How unloving would that be? How out of character would that be for a God Who is love? We must understand that God's bidding is God's enabling. He will never call us to be what He will not empower us to be. God only comes to us in love, and this God, Who is love, says to us today, what He has been saying to us all our lives:

> "Come to me, all you who are weary and burdened, and I will give you rest. Take my yoke upon you and learn from me, for I am gentle and humble in heart, and you will find rest for your souls. For my yoke is easy and my burden is light." (Matthew 11:28-30)

If we take Him at His word and come to Him, not just once, not just at special times in our journey, but every moment of every day, then we will find rest and we will understand that in Christ, the yoke is actually easy and the burden is actually light. Jesus was not tricking us or lying to us or talking in cryptic language which needs to be interpreted by some scholar. This God, Who is love, appeals to us every day of our lives to not be anxious, not be fearful, not be afraid - but to throw ourselves upon Him afresh and learn from Him and trust Him.

So regardless of what we think causes fear or anxiety in our lives, at the base of it all is the sin of unbelief. We just don't want to accept responsibility for something which we can blame on others. But until we do, we will never be free.

If we don't take responsibility for everything in our life, nothing will change. Our focus should never be on our fears – that only empowers them. Fear is not the problem – our unbelief is the problem - and that, we can fix, with help from the Holy Spirit. We simply need to join the father of that demon-possessed boy in Mark 9:24 who stood before Jesus and said, "Lord, I believe – help me in my unbelief."

God longs to hear that prayer from us because God knows how amazing our lives will be when we actually believe Him, trust Him and allow Him to fill us to the measure of all His fullness.

But as long as we see ourselves as a victim; as long as it's somebody else's fault we feel this way or act this way or have to live this way; as long as we continue to blame somebody else for what ultimately is our problem; as long as we point the finger of accusation to someone else and say, *"You made me feel this way ..."* then we will never know, this side of the grave, what it is to be filled to the measure of all the fullness of God.

God's love drives out all fear, but those are just words on a page and hot air from a preacher until you *believe* them and receive them as a promise from God. God loves you. God cares for you, and when you fear or doubt, you are really saying to God, *"I don't trust you. I don't believe You have really done what You say or will do what You've promised to do."*

That's why unbelief is a hideous sin and that's why we need to confess it, repent of it and embrace the Truth. That Truth is Jesus, given to us, given for us and in Him we now live and in Him we can and we will be free from all guilt; free from all shame; free from the sting of accusation; free from all punishment; free from the penalty and power of sin, free from anxiety; free from a victim mentality; free from all fear!

I invite you to pray a prayer with me now and perhaps many more times in the days ahead. I have based this prayer on that amazing Psalm 23 which I hope some of you read every night this past week as suggested.

I encourage you to really believe these words and expect God to answer this prayer in your life.

Why don't you pray this we me now:

Lord, I believe … You really are my shepherd and I shall not want for anything.

Lord, I believe …You will make me lie down in green pastures, and lead me beside quiet waters, and restore my soul.

Lord, I believe … You will guide me in paths of righteousness for Your name's sake.

Lord, I believe … that even though I walk through the valley of the shadow of death, I will fear no evil, for I believe You are with me; Your rod and your staff, will comfort me.

Lord, I believe …You are preparing a table before me in the presence of my enemies and You will anoint my head with oil.

Lord, I believe …You when You promise that my cup will overflow.

Lord, I believe … that goodness and love (not fear and anxiety) will follow me all the days of my life

Lord, I believe … I will dwell in Your house forever.

Lord, I believe … now help me in my unbelief.

In Jesus' mighty name I pray, Amen

CHAPTER EIGHT
Without Love it's all Nothing!

The giving and receiving of love lie at the foundation of our lives and if we are to become truly successful in life, we need to learn how to receive love and give love. We can pursue success and fulfilment in any other area of life - but if we miss out on being loved by God and others and returning that love to God and others - then we will have missed the whole reason for being created.

In this chapter I will draw your attention to that beautiful 'hymn of love' in 1 Corinthians 13. Paul's famous ode to love is well known and it's often read at weddings. Any passage on love is appropriate to read at a wedding - including this one. However, to see this passage only in that context is to miss the whole point which Paul wanted to make when he wrote these powerful words.

If you read this whole letter to the Christians at Corinth you will see Paul is scolding these believers because of their silly, air-head spiritual ways. In that context what he then effectively says in chapter 13 is: *"You can look and sound spiritual and do all sorts of things in Jesus' name - but without love - it's all nothing!"*

Therefore, this beautiful passage was a stern correction to the abuse and sinful behaviour in that Church and a strong reminder that love is at the heart of any God-honouring ministry or life.

The presence or absence of love is the ultimate test of authenticity in the church. If this passage is going to have any relevance for us, we first need to hear it and experience it in its original context.

The Corinthian believers had elevated one spiritual gift above the others. That gift was speaking in tongues and they had effectively made this one spiritual gift the mark of true spirituality and they were not the last Christians to make that mistake. In doing this, they had neglected and even downplayed common decency, courtesy, servility and genuine, selfless love. These believers got the idea that if they had any kind of spiritual experience then it was good, and if it was weird and out of the ordinary – then even better! Paul tells them they are way off the track.

Paul clearly says in a number of places in this letter to the Corinthian church that just being spiritual; just having a spiritual experience and even exercising a true spiritual gift is not necessarily a good thing. If that gift is not exercised in a way that is helpful to people; if it's not edifying to people, then we are not operating in love. Paul doesn't downplay the gifts themselves - he just stresses that love must be the vehicle in which those gifts travel within the Body of Christ and out into the community around us.

The key to knowing how to act in a church community is whether it helps people. Are people loved or encouraged or blessed or edified or built up as a result of that ministry? In Paul's mind, spirituality boils down to something very basic; something that we all need to understand, appreciate and be reminded of often.

God's love must be the fuel in our tanks, the grease on our axles and our spiritual GPS. That is the essence of what Paul says in this very beautiful, but quite confronting chapter. Being religious or spiritual doesn't impress God. He doesn't care for religion. He doesn't care about the survival of a particular ministry. What God is really concerned about is that people are helped and that His love is flowing through us to everyone around us. That is the only business God is in - because God is love.

Therefore, when we exercise the gifts God has imparted to the church in the context of love; when we channel them into helping people, then, and only then, are they valid in a ministry context.

Paul's first letter to the Corinthian believers was written to correct them and to guide them out of their spiritual silliness and immaturity because people were not being loved, helped or respected.

Today we must be reminded that 1 Corinthians 13 is more than a beautiful description of love – it's a confronting challenge to us all and, if needed, a sobering rebuke. It should force us to look at our behaviour and the exercising of our gifts so we can ensure that the wonderful qualities of love, as given to us by God, are manifested in the way we live and act inside and outside the Church.

Let's just look at the first few verses of this reading:

> *"If I speak in the tongues of men or of angels, but do not have love, I am only a resounding gong or a clanging cymbal. If I have the gift of prophecy and can fathom all mysteries and all knowledge, and if I have a faith that can move mountains, but do not have love, I am nothing. If I give all I possess to the poor and give over my body to hardship that I may boast, but do not have love, I gain nothing." (1 Corinthians 13:1-3)*

Now Paul intentionally starts by talking about tongues and prophecy because these were two of the gifts which were being abused in the Corinthian church. If we read on into chapter 14 of this letter he deals with this abuse in detail. But his point here is simple: if the way you operate as believers is not lovingly focused on those unbelievers whom you desire to see come to Christ, then you have missed the mark.

Paul says that when unbelievers come into our gatherings and see and hear things they simply cannot understand or relate to, then it will do them no good whatsoever - it will probably guarantee that you never see some of them again. Unless someone has been able to explain what is happening and turn something which appears weird into something edifying for all, then they will not be helped. Therefore, Paul says, *don't do it!*

Now of course there will always be some things that need explanation and things which are spiritually discerned once those people are enlightened by the Holy Spirit. Generally speaking, however, the unbeliever should be able to get a grasp on what's happening fairly quickly in a way that makes sense to them and is a blessing to them and leads them towards God, rather than drive them away in confusion or fear and in some cases – just pure boredom!

That's one of the reasons why I try to preach as simply and as clearly as I can and I have received positive feedback from many outside the church to my teaching over the years which is encouraging and continues to keep me as grounded as possible in the way I present the gospel. I hope I will always preach that way and I hope the church will always minister that way.

That doesn't mean God can't manifest His presence in ways that none of us understand - it just means that as far as it depends on us - we should ensure that there is a simple, clear proclamation of who we are, Whose we are and why we are here – demonstrated by what we say, what we do and how we live … all of that is lubricated, saturated and motivated by love.

It would seem that the Corinthians had lost sight of this. Paul doesn't criticise them for speaking in tongues. He doesn't infer that it wasn't a genuine spiritual gift.

Paul simply says that they were exercising this gift in a way that God never intended and so it was not helpful and therefore not loving - and if it's not done in love, then it amounts to nothing! We need to get the strength of this. Paul says that a genuine spiritual gift from God, if it's being exercised in a way that does not help anyone - if it's done without love - then it's absolutely worthless. That's a very strong, but really important statement.

Love is always more important than religious activity. Love is always more important than abstract spirituality. People are more important than ministry programs. You can see this throughout the ministry of Jesus. He demonstrated this truth every day He was among us. The best examples were when Jesus healed people on the Sabbath. Every time He healed someone on the Sabbath, the religious people were there ready to tell Him, *"You can't do that, Jesus. That's not spiritual. That's not right. Haven't you read the Old Testament where is says not to work on the Sabbath?"*

Well, of course Jesus knew the Old Testament better than any of these amateurs and so He told them in word and in deed that people are more important than their skewed interpretation of the law. Love always triumphs over religion.

Jesus always put people and their real needs ahead of spirituality or religious practices. So, our spiritual activities might be good - they might even be supernatural in the sense that we normally use that word, but they all amount to nothing if people are not cared for; if they are not served in some way; if they are not truly loved.

Then Paul goes on to explain what this loving and self-giving and helpfulness actually looks like and these are the verses we remember so well – and rightly so.

> *"Love is patient, love is kind. It does not envy, it does not boast, it is not proud. It does not dishonour others, it is not self-seeking, it is not easily angered, it keeps no record of wrongs. Love does not delight in evil but "rejoices with the truth. It always protects, always trusts, always hopes, always perseveres. Love never fails. But where there are prophecies, they will cease; where there are tongues, they will be stilled; where there is knowledge, it will pass away."*
> *(1 Corinthians 13:4-8)*

Notice that these statements are all relational in nature. Love serves the real needs of people, in contrast with the modern feeling of love, which is that it's only a feeling, just an emotion. The New Testament would not understand that concept of love. That's why for us today in our culture it's hard to read in the English translation the word 'love' and even begin to know what it means because our frame of reference for that word has shifted a long way from Paul's frame of reference. Love for us in our culture is often a warm mushy feeling we have. In this passage love is still a feeling – but it's also an act of our will - it's a verb – it's something that we do. People see our love in action ... or not.

These Corinthians thought they were a cut above the average because they had some pretty flashy supernatural gifts in operation. Paul then cuts them down to size when he says:

> *"... where there are prophecies, they will cease; where there are tongues, they will be stilled; where there is knowledge, it will pass away."*

They were boasting that they had it all, and Paul was telling them they actually had nothing! This must have been quite a shock to these believers.

Paul was pointing out the selfish attitudes of some people in that church who were hell-bent on getting everything for themselves. Paul says love is patient and kind and you are not – and that effectively renders you a big spiritual zero. You can see why I get a little uneasy reading this passage at wedding ceremonies - when I understand it's original context. It's a hard word of rebuke and warning and it's also a very necessary word for today.

Now I could unpack this love chapter word by word but that's not necessary in this context. It is self-explanatory. It contains the clearest language we will find anywhere in the New Testament and once we understand the central point that Paul is trying to make - the whole chapter rings with clarity and power. We must then look in the mirror and ask some hard questions as we evaluate our lives, our ministries and the whole church against this benchmark of love.

When we look at this standard and see our shortcomings, we shouldn't rate ourselves or others. This is not meant to induce guilt or judgement. We are 100% accepted in Christ, regardless of our performance. It is on the basis of Christ's perfect performance that we are now accepted. We can't do anything good enough to be more accepted by God and we can't do anything bad enough to be less accepted by God. Our acceptance is complete in Christ and in Christ there is no condemnation.

Having said that, our daily lives are transformed when we identify and address our shortcomings and, in that process, our effectiveness as ministers of the Gospel is then greatly enhanced.

If we look at these lofty ideals in 1 Corinthians 13 honestly and allow some self-assessment and healthy repentance to flow - we can grow in a beautiful way.

Better still, we also get to read this passage as a glorious promise of where we are headed and who we are becoming in Christ.

The New Testament tells us that God is love and in 1 Corinthians 13, Paul gives us a long description of what love looks like and acts like, thereby giving us one of the most accurate and beautiful descriptions of the God we serve. If God is love, then this is what we can also read:

> *"God is patient, God is kind. God does not envy, God does not boast, God is not proud. God does not dishonour others, God is not self-seeking, God is not easily angered, God keeps no record of wrongs. God does not delight in evil but rejoices with the truth. God always protects, always trusts, always hopes, always perseveres. God never fails."*

Can you now see why God is the perfect person to live with? How would you like to be married to someone like that? Wouldn't that be great? Well, that is who God is. For many people in our world that comes as a surprise because they may have grown up with an understanding of God that is different to that.

Regardless of how you feel about God; regardless of how unhappy you think He might be with you, I can assure you on the authority of Scripture and personal experience over my whole life that God is all of the above and more.

Wouldn't it be nice if you were married to someone who never remembered what you did wrong the day before? Think about that for a moment. The fact of the matter is, you are married to such a person. Everyone who believes in the Lord Jesus Christ, has entered into an intimate relationship with God Himself, the God Who keeps no record of wrongs. Think how the Church would look if today, if right now, we all stopped keeping a record of each other's wrongs.

What would the Church look like if we all wiped the slate clean and looked at tomorrow, not yesterday, in all our relationships? My mind cannot conceive the glory of such a thing. But that is how God operates every day with each one of us and we miss it because we don't believe the truth of Who God is, or because we're too busy recording everybody else's wrongs or dwelling on our own failures, so we don't have time to bask in God's accepting, forgiving, love.

The word in the Greek behind that phrase in verse 5 is the same term used to refer to bookkeeping. Literally translated it means: *'Love does not compile statistics of wrong - love does not keep score.'*

Some people still believe that they are going wake up one cold morning in heaven and for a while they are going to wish they hadn't because their whole life is going to be played out on some big screen before them. All of their sins - all of those things done in secret - all up there for everyone to see. I was actually taught that in Sunday School. One of my children was told that in a devotions one morning by her teacher at a Christian School. That is not the truth (and my daughter stood up in class and told the teacher he was wrong). It says so right here. *Love keeps no record of wrongs and God is love.* How much clearer can we make it?

In Hebrews 8:12 we read that in the new covenant - in New Testament Christianity, God says, *"I will remember their sins no more!"* You cannot get any clearer than that. When God says, *"Forget it,"* that's exactly what He means! There is no permanent record to be used against us later and what that means is that since God doesn't hold it against us, we can off-load the guilt and the shame and start fresh every day. We don't need to live with the aggravation and pain and humiliation of the sins we have committed in the past - God keeps no record of our wrongs – so why should we?

The more we accept the truth; drink in His unconditional love and complete forgiveness; the more we will become like God and the less inclined we will be to keep a record of other people's wrongs. When we experience the reality of God's forgiveness and the clean slate He gives us every day - we will be better empowered to do the same to others.

Then, we will start to see the power of God's love explode in the midst of congregations across our nation; then, the gospel will actually be good news again and people will be drawn to it like they always have when our God, Who is love, is revealed to them free from all the religious nonsense which has camouflaged and redefined Him for generations. As that happens, then that powerful prayer of Jesus we have recorded in John 17 will finally be answered, for it was Jesus Himself Who prayed to the Father and said:

> *"I have made you known to them, and will continue to make you known in order that the love you have for me may be in them and that I myself may be in them." (John 17:26)*

The only human being ever to walk this planet who truly loved people with the heart and love of God was Jesus, and now, through the mystery of God's amazing grace, it is in Christ we live and move and have our being. That is the only reason we can love anyone, because it is the love of God in Christ which constrains us, empowers us, renews us and propels us towards a lost and needy world, confident that love never fails, because God never fails.

I want to finish this chapter by doing something which may or may not work remotely via this medium. But then again it might work better than if we were all in the same room. I want you to use your imagination here. I want to remind you of the qualities of God, Who is love, but I also want to remind you of who you are becoming in Christ as you are slowly being transformed into His image.

1 Corinthians 13 explains true love to us but as I said before, it also reveals God to us. But even more than that, it reveals who we are and who we are becoming in Christ. I want you to imagine that I am standing before God right now and I am asking God to describe you. That's right, I want God to tell me about you.

I want God to describe what He sees in you and who He believes you are. I want you to 'listen' in your spirit now to how God describes what He sees in you. This is who you really are in Christ, right now. When I ask God to describe you, these are the words He uses:

Patient. Kind. Content. Humble. Honouring. Unselfish. Peaceful. Forgiving. Truthful. Caring. Protecting. Trusting. Hoping. Enduring. Unfailing.

Perhaps you are struggling to receive some of those words of affirmation because you know you're not all those things most days. You know your shortcomings, your failings, your sin. So how could those words describe you? The answer is simple.

The answer is Jesus. Jesus Christ is the reason God sees all those things in you because Christ is in you and you are in Christ and the more you submit to the work of His Spirit in you the more you will be transformed into the image of the One Who has given you all of this for free, by His grace.

1 Corinthians 13 contains many things. It contains a strong rebuke to those who claim to live in Christ but act in ways which betray Him. It contains a glorious description of true love and because God is love, it also contains a glorious description of God. However, this wonderful passage also contains a glorious description of you as you now stand in Christ. God sees all those things in you, even if you don't.

So, when you decide to believe that this is who you really are becoming in Christ; when you make choices each day which are then consistent with this view of you, then your life will be transformed and people around you will be drawn to the life within you – they will be drawn to Jesus. People are always drawn to Jesus!

Let those who have ears to hear, listen to what the Spirit of God is saying to us all right now.

CHAPTER NINE
Acceptance and Change

As we continue this foundational teaching on love, we are going to look at Paul's whole letter to the Ephesians over the next couple of chapters - not in detail – just an overview. As we do that, we will discover that there is a progression in Paul's references to love and a powerful presentation of the Gospel at the same time. Before we look at this in more detail, allow me to give you a quick 'fly-over' view of that progression.

In Ephesians 1, we learn that God has sovereignly chosen us - to love us. That is, as I've said before, God created us in love - for love. Our primary purpose in life is to have a loving relationship with God and in turn with those around us. It doesn't matter what else we are good at – if we blow this - we've blown life!

But if we do manage to get it together with God this side of the grave and learn how to receive and give His love and we don't do anything else terribly well, then my Bible tells me we are still a roaring success!

On the flip side, we could achieve amazing things in this life - earn multiple degrees or win a Nobel prize or cure the world of some disease - but if we miss out on receiving and giving love, then that same Bible tells me we have missed the entire point of our life and our achievements mean nothing in the Kingdom of God.

God chose us in love, for love. This is the perfect declaration of God's grace: Before we were good or bad; before we looked for or wanted God; before we had any sense of need for God; before we even knew how to spell the word repent; before we were even born, in fact, *God chose us.*

God's love comes to us as His free, sovereign choice because it's God's nature to love. It has nothing to do with us, initially. All love in this sinful, fallen world is conditional. Even the purest of human love has a price tag - but God's love has no price tag. God's love is free. It has no strings attached. It is unconditional. We don't have to be good enough or spiritual enough to earn His love.

Moving along in the progression, in Ephesians 2, God's sovereign love is not just His choosing of us; it's not just His affection for us; it's also His power in us. The love of God doesn't just assure us that He feels warm and fuzzy towards us - God's love is effective. It's something that impacts us and does something to us, in us and through us. It changes us. You cannot be impacted by the love of God and not be transformed in some way.

In Ephesians 3, Paul calls us to now become rooted and grounded in this free, sovereign love, which has made us alive in Christ. Do you see the progression? God chose us and loves us, but not just that; His love impacts our lives, but not just that; now that we have this love that has affected us, we are to be rooted and grounded in it. We are to wrestle with it and meditate upon it and rest in it and lay the foundation of our lives upon it. That's the third aspect of this progression.

The next one is in Ephesians 4. Paul explains that this love of God which has come to us personally and made us alive as individuals, and in which we are to become established, rooted and grounded, though it is personal – it's not private - it's also for the Body of Christ - the church. Out of love we are to speak to each other and build each other up so that the Body of Christ will be healthy and effective. That is to say, the love of God is not our personal property or for our experience only.

All spiritual experience in Christ is not supposed to stop with us - it is meant to flow through us. Of course, God's love is meant to affect us, bring us joy, bring us power, bring us life - but it's not complete until it has been passed on, given away and channelled into someone else's life. It's to be passed on first of all to the church – to our brothers and sisters in Christ. But it's not meant to stop there either. Sadly, it does, more often than not, but Ephesians 5 tells us this love needs to be passed on to the whole world. That's why John 3:16 does <u>not</u> say *"God so loved <u>the church</u> that He gave His only Son …"* It says, *"For God so loved <u>the world</u> ..."*

The love that God lavishes upon us doesn't just make us alive, but through us, it is the instrument God uses to make other people alive as well. This progression, which moves through the book of Ephesians, perfectly describes how God's love affects us and matures its expression in us and through us to those around us.

So in this chapter and the next, I want to talk about the first few stages in this progression of love and give us a chance to assess ourselves to see where we are in this process - to see if we have stumbled or tripped or stalled at some point in that process and then give the Holy Spirit the chance to take us deeper in one or all of these areas. And to do that, we are going to stop and pray at certain times.

This is where we can get in touch with our heart; connect with the Holy Spirit within us; and ask for discernment to assess where we are in this progression. This is important. In fact, if I truly believe what I have been writing in this book on love and if you have believed anything you have read, then I would suggest that this is all that really matters in our life. If we get love right - then we've made it in this life and everything else will fall into place. If we miss this, then we've missed it all. Ok, back to the text:

*"Praise be to the God and Father of our Lord Jesus Christ,
who has blessed us in the heavenly realms with every
spiritual blessing in Christ. For he chose us in him before the
creation of the world to be holy and blameless in his sight. In
love he predestined us for adoption as his children through
Jesus Christ, in accordance with his pleasure and will - to
the praise of his glorious grace, which he has freely given us
in the One he loves." (Ephesians 1:3-6)*

Notice the key reference to love here. Paul, the Apostle, the
great theologian and a genius to many in the ancient world,
says that the focus of all knowledge and truth is love. God
first of all chose us for Himself in love and He did it before
creation. He did it before we were good, before we were
bad, before we cared about God at all - He chose us.

People might say: *"I sought God and I found Him .."* and that
is certainly how it feels from our end. But strictly speaking,
God sought and found us before we were even born and it's
a free sovereign choice, but it's not a choice which is devoid
of emotion. Many preachers and theologians have tried for
years to downplay feelings and take the emotion out of God
and out of our relationship with God. Yet you cannot read
the Bible and say that God is not emotional. The word for
love that we find here in Ephesians is a love which is self-
giving; a love that is disciplined and it will hang in there
through thick and thin.

All that is true, but it is also a love that carries with it a deep
and warm affection. There is a strong emotional component
to this love. Just like a mother can be emotionally attached
to and affectionate towards a baby that's not even born yet
- so too God can be affectionate towards us in the womb of
His heart long before we were born in this world. Before the
creation of the world God loved us and chose us in love, but
as Paul points out it was not just out of His good will but
His pleasure also.

It was pleasurable for Him to see us, to delight in us and to choose us before we were even born. This is grace. This is the free sovereign love of God.

It doesn't really matter how many times we have heard this truth preached, we can never hear it too often! We need this truth to be burned into our mind. Before we did anything to earn it or deserve it, God loved us. This is all God's work. When were you saved? The Bible says you were saved before the foundation of the world in the heart of a God Who is love, a God Who loved you and saved you and made you alive in Christ - in His perfect plan and purpose - before you even knew God existed.

In fact, before you even entered this world yourself. That's when you were related to God and this God is committed to you in love by an act of His will and He will be true to that commitment forever.

But there's more … God is also crazy about you! God gets warm fuzzies when He thinks about you. God delights in your presence. God takes joy in just being with you. I know that's hard for some of you to receive, but it happens to be true. OK – it's time to pause, to discern, to respond and to pray. Ponder these questions:

Are you convinced that you have been loved and accepted by God? Are you convinced that God chose you before you did anything good or bad? Are you convinced that you are a delight to God and that He has pledged Himself to you personally for eternity, regardless of your performance? Do you really know that truth deep in your heart today – the truth that truly will set you gloriously and powerfully free forever?

Are you absolutely, completely convinced of that? Many of you may be. Praise God! Some of you may not be.

So let me pray this prayer over you, confident that God can answer this prayer wherever you are and whenever you read this. You may even like to pray this with me …

> *Holy Spirit of God, show us our hearts now and if any of us are not totally convinced of God's overwhelming and unconditional love for us today, then I simply ask that You will move in power right now and touch the hearts and minds and lives of everyone reading this now. In Jesus' mighty name, bring a glorious and fresh revelation of truth into each and every life and may we move forward from this day with no doubt whatsoever of Your love.*

> *May each of us know today and always that the reason You love us, has everything to do with Who You are and nothing to do with Who we are or how we perform. You love us because You choose to love us. You enjoy loving us and always have loved us. Come, Holy Spirit and saturate our spirits with this life-changing truth – this good news – this gospel. In Jesus name, amen.*

Now in addition to God choosing us, this love of His is not static. It is not just a declaration of His attitude towards us. It is something that powerfully affects us. Let's move on in this progression in Ephesians.

> *"But because of his great love for us, God, who is rich in mercy, made us alive with Christ even when we were dead in our sins - it is by grace you have been saved."*
> *(Ephesians 2:4-5)*

Do you remember the KFC Hot & Spicy advertisements on television a few years ago where a guy sinks his teeth into a chicken burger and his mate across the table slaps him on both sides of the face – symbolising the power and impact of this amazing spicy meal?

Well, when I read this powerful sentence from the Apostle Paul, this amazing truth, this gospel diamond … I feel slapped in the face, in love of course. So let me state this truth again in the clearest way I know as you listen in your spirit:

"When you were DEAD in your sins,
GOD MADE YOU ALIVE with Christ!"

This is the heart and soul of the entire New Testament. This is the foundation of our Christian faith. This is the bedrock upon which all doctrine must be built. This is the window through which we must view all other Scriptures. This is the essence of God's plan of salvation. This is what God's love looks like up close and personal.

God's love is not just a feeling; not just an emotion; not just His affection toward us since the foundation of the world; it's all those things but God's love is also an action – it is effective – it is powerful - it achieves a purpose beyond itself – it is focussed on the transformation of the recipients.

We humans are pretty complex creatures. There's a lot to sort out before we really understand ourselves or others. However, when we drill down through all our differences and idiosyncrasies and the things that make us unique, we will find the same emotional and spiritual DNA.

We are all the same when it comes to what we need and want more than anything else in the world. I want to tell you what that is today. In my humble opinion, there are two things which every human being wants and needs more than anything else on the periphery of their lives – just two and they form the title of this chapter:

Acceptance and change.

We all want to be accepted, don't we? Those people in our lives who have truly loved us; the ones from whom we really have felt genuine love, will be the ones who accepted us as we are. They knew all our shortcomings and loved us anyway. That's what we want. We don't want to have to follow someone's rules or fulfil someone's expectations in order to be accepted. That's why deep down we all hate religion – because that's what religion expects. If you are caught up in religion, then you know exactly what you have to do or have to be before you are accepted or honoured or considered worthy. But no matter how sincere and devoted you are within that religion, there is something deep within you which is crying out, *"No! I don't want to have to perform or conform or behave in a certain way in order to be loved and accepted by God or God's people!"*

Well, I have some really great news for you! That acceptance we long for; that unconditional, no-need-to-jump-through-any-religious-hoops acceptance we crave and need is given to us freely in the Gospel! We are 100% accepted by God regardless of anything we do or don't do! Only the Gospel, only the good news of God, in Christ can meet one of the most basic and important human needs: *acceptance.*

But humans are a paradox! Whilst we desperately need to be accepted as we are and not expected to change in order to earn God's love or the love of His people – deep down we actually don't want to stay as we are! We are just as desperate in our need for *change.* We actually want to change. We want to grow. We want to mature but we don't want to be forced to do so in order to earn the acceptance of others or of God.

Enter again: the life-changing good news – the Gospel in Christ! God accepts us totally as we are, but He loves us too much to leave us there!

God's love is not static. God's love is dynamic. It impacts us. It changes us. It leads us to repentance. It gives us life as God intended us to have – abundant life! This is what God is all about and this is what the church should be all about. *Acceptance and change.*

First and foremost, God has accepted us, in spite of us, regardless of our performance, our obedience, our devotion or our service. He has chosen us before the foundation of the world. Therefore, we have no right to beat ourselves up in guilt and shame and we have no right to reject others.

We are called to accept each other in Christ because God accepts us in Christ. We don't condone sinful behaviour in others, but we accept the sinner in the same way God accepts them - as they are – regardless of their lifestyle or their behaviour or their appearance.

Now here is the key to real church growth - here is the essence of the Ministry of Jesus Christ - it is this genuine, unconditional, God-inspired acceptance of others – as they are – where they are – how they are, which will bring the power of God's love into their lives and bring about the transformation we desire to see in them; the change which they desire deep down but are just incapable of achieving without God's love at work in their lives.

God's heart has been broken millions and millions and millions of times over hundreds of years now as He has watched the visible church which bears the name of Christ effectively ask God's chosen children to change, to repent, to be something they are not at present, *before* they can truly connect to the life of Jesus Christ in His church or before they feel like they belong or are accepted as equals before God. There are some church congregations which still do this deliberately and without apology.

They believe their mission is to call people to repentance first and love them second and in so doing, they make it very clear what is moral and immoral; what is acceptable and unacceptable behaviour; what lifestyle honours God and what dishonours God.

Then there are countless other congregations which don't deliberately set out to put conditions and qualifying criteria on God's love, but by default, we end up singing from the same hymn sheet and the world learns very quickly that the entry criteria for the Christian church is very clear: You need to act a certain way, refrain from acting in other ways, and subscribe to a certain stated or implied code of conduct or belief system to fit in or be loved, accepted or respected as a child of Almighty God.

Is it any wonder that we have Christian leaders all over the world scratching their heads wondering why the Gospel is not bearing fruit as Paul promised it always would when we understand grace in all its truth? (Colossians 1:6). This 'gospel' is not bearing fruit because it's not the true Gospel at all! It is a legalistic, demonically inspired corruption of the truth which is actually designed to cripple the church and continually portray to the world a God Who is anything but love!

Therefore, in this second stage in our progression through Ephesians, we really need some discernment and we really need the Truth of the Gospel, and nothing but the Truth to impregnate, to saturate, to overwhelm us to the point where we are 100% sure and unquestionably clear that our God, Who is love, accepts us totally and unconditionally in Jesus Christ and always will. We must be equally clear and that it is this total acceptance and unconditional love which births repentance, transformation and change in our lives.

I invite you to pray with me again now …

Lord God, release Your Holy Spirit within us afresh right now. Reveal to our mind and our heart who we are in relationship to You. We pray also Lord that You would help us see areas of our lives that still need more of Your life-giving love. Help us Lord to be honest and fearless in holding them up before You in the days ahead. If there is any religion left in us – reveal it and remove it, Lord.

If our image of You and Your love and Your church and our mission in Christ has in any way been taken hostage by Satan, by legalism, by religion, by the 'do-more-try-harder-to-please-God' forces which have crippled millions of your children and countless churches, then reveal it to us now and give us the courage to let it all go and be overwhelmed once more by the power of Your love, by the glory of Your Gospel of grace and by the freedom which is ours in Christ.

Lord, help us to see what You see in us and may that revelation transform us in our relationship with You and in our relationship and commitment to Your church and in our relationship and attitude to those outside the church who are yet to really hear the Gospel, yet to really encounter their God, Who is love. We ask this in the mighty and matchless name of Jesus, Amen.

CHAPTER TEN
The Outrageous Love of God

We have been looking at this amazing progression in Paul's references to love in his letter to the Ephesians. In chapter one we saw that God sovereignly chooses us. God created us in love - for love. Our primary purpose in life is to have a loving relationship with God and then, in turn, with those around us.

Then in chapter two of Ephesians, we saw that God's sovereign love is not just His choosing of us; it's not just His affection for us; it is also His power within us. His love impacts us and actually does something to us, in us and through us. The love of God affects our being. You cannot be truly impacted by God' love and remain the same. For many years I had the following statement on my desk to remind me of this truth:

God sees all that you should be
God sees all that you could be
But God loves you, just as you are

Religion is very concerned about what you *should* be and many churches are passionate to tell you what you *could* be, but God simply comes to you in love, *just as you are*. However, when that amazing truth, God's amazing grace, really sinks in and God's unconditional love impacts you deep down in your soul, then a transformation will begin and it continues and intensifies day by day. The more you drink in the unconditional love and grace of God; the more you embrace the empowering presence of God, then the more you become all that you *could* be and all that you *should* be! This is the Gospel! This is the good news in Jesus Christ. This is why we are still here!

Let's move on now in this natural progression of love which Paul gives us in Ephesians, as we enter chapter three. Now that we have been chosen and loved by God and this love has affected us in life-changing ways, this is where we are to stay at all times - rooted and established or grounded in that love. We don't move on from that reality. We don't grow out of our need for God's love. We don't 'mature' into some place in our relationship with God where we don't need His empowering presence and love. We need to be rooted and grounded in what God has done for us every day and it's out of that reality that we then minister and do things for God and with God in the world around us.

> *"I pray that out of his glorious riches he may strengthen you with power through his Spirit in your inner being, so that Christ may dwell in your hearts through faith. And I pray that you, being rooted and established in love, may have power, together with all the Lord's holy people, to grasp how wide and long and high and deep is the love of Christ, and to know this love that surpasses knowledge - that you may be filled to the measure of all the fullness of God."*
> *(Ephesians 3:16-19)*

When I first embraced my salvation personally and started living for God, I read a lot of books and I heard a lot of teaching about what I needed to now do as a new believer and what I needed to be grounded in so I could be strong and effective for God. I had quite a list! Now these were very helpful things.

I was told to read the Bible and pray and commit to a church family and give my money, time and gifts; to share my faith with others and to support overseas missionaries … to name just a few! All these things were important and all the advice I was given no doubt came with love and the best of intentions.

However, someone forgot to tell me the most important thing! Something vitally important and foundational was missing, or so well-disguised that I have no recollection of it. None of those books said that before you do anything else by way of Christian activity or service or spiritual discipline – first and foremost, you must be rooted and grounded in God's love. That is the foundation. There is where you need to drop anchor first. You need to grow deep roots into God's love before you do anything else. Everything must flow out of that reservoir of God's love in your life.

Sadly, I was one of millions of disciples who were not really told the most important truth of all, which is that all of those wonderful acts of worship; all of those precious spiritual disciplines and Christian activities and service are actually meant to be the fruit of something more foundational, and more important. None of those things are worth anything unless they are the fruit of God's empowering presence, God's amazing grace, God's overwhelming, lavish love in our lives. Our life must be first established in God and His finished work in Christ, before we can participate in life with our worship, our good works or our service.

I've noticed in Sydney over recent years, as available land for building is swallowed up, that they are using a lot of swamp land to build on. Now this can be done - if it's done correctly. They build it all up to get it out of the swamp, but first, they must drill down through the mud, the swamp and the shifting sand until they hit bedrock and then they drive these multiple steel cylinders down and fill them with concrete, just like I saw them doing a few years ago in the middle of the Clarence river for the new Harwood Bridge on the far north coast of NSW. Whether its swamp land, low lying flood planes or even in the middle of our largest river on the east coast – you can build anything you like as long as you have that rock-solid foundation firmly in place.

Now, you can probably imagine them drilling through the swamp or the mud, can't you? Someone would yell, *'Have we hit rock yet?'... no? Go deeper then ... have we hit rock yet?' 'Yes? Excellent, now we can build.'* Until they hit that bedrock, any construction would be futile, or worse than that, the building may go ahead and look great for a while until one day the pressure on that structure is just too great and the absence of a rock-solid foundation will result in a disaster – like in that Canadian house I told you about earlier.

In Jesus' name, hear God's Word to us again today: God's love is that bedrock in our lives, in our ministries, in our congregations and in the entire church across the world. We should always be asking as we build our lives and help Jesus build His church:

Have we hit rock yet?
Have we hit God's love yet?
Do we understand God's love yet?
Have we been affected by God's love yet?
Have we felt God's love yet?
Do we really know the magnitude of God's love yet?

Until we are overwhelmed by, saturated in, and firmly rooted in and grounded upon the love of God, we actually haven't hit rock yet and any building we do without that foundation in place will be careless and doomed to crumble eventually.

It may fail when we are young as the pressures of our peer group lead us astray. It may fail in middle age when the pressures of family and work reach their peak. It may fail in our twilight years when death approaches and we are finally forced to examine the foundation of our faith and the reality of our personal relationship with God.

God's love for us in Christ is the bedrock of the abundant Christian life and everything else is built upon that love. So, let me ask you now, have you drilled down past your own efforts, past your many successes and failures, to reach the bedrock of God's love? Have you drilled down past your own commitments, past your own holiness, your own righteousness and, for that matter, your own sin, and found the rock of God's love and grace yet?

So many Christians were never told just how important this is and they have built their lives on faulty foundations and now we have all kinds of bad attitudes and practices and wonky theology across the church and this image of a Christian which the world does not find attractive at all … because too many people never drilled down far enough to hit that bedrock of gospel truth.

My passion, my calling, my life's work, my deepest desire is that we do this right for the next generation of believers and the only way that will happen is for the Gospel of God's amazing grace and love to be preached like the Apostle Paul preached it, over and over and over and over again. Still today, millions of new believers in Christ are given a list of behaviours and disciplines which they need to embrace before they are treated like loved and accepted members of the church. That's not the Christian faith - that's religion and God hates religion with a passion!

What God wants and longs for is a free relationship of love and trust and the more we drink in God's unconditional love, the more empowered we will be to live the life God is calling us to live. A free relationship of love - not one which try to purchase with our obedience, or our confession, or our repentance, or our diligent service - but a radically free relationship. How free? Let me tell you how radically free God's love is to you today.

I want you to picture Jesus hanging on the cross, near death, writhing in agony, spiritually crushed by the weight of the sin of the world ... and then the most extraordinary thing happens. With His dying breath, Jesus has a conversation with the thief on the next cross.

This brief snapshot at the end of Jesus' earthly life showcases the radical Gospel of God's grace and love in just one paragraph – one picture – one brief encounter with one broken human being.

In the last minutes of his life this criminal encounters the love of God nailed to the cross beside him and this low-life says the most arrogant, infuriating thing a religious person would ever want to hear leave the mouth of this scumbag ... he turned to Jesus and said, *"Jesus, remember me when you come into your kingdom."*

Then from the next cross comes the essence of our whole faith, the Gospel, the bedrock of the church, the simplicity of the good news: Love then turns His bloodied, tortured face towards this low-life criminal who deserves everything he's getting and says, *"Today, you will be with me in paradise."*

Outrageous! Unbelievable! How could this be? asks every Pharisee who ever lived! Did this thief tick any of the boxes which religion requires? Did he repent? Did he confess his sins? Was he baptised? Did he study his Bible? Did he pray, visit the sick, give a tenth of his income or serve in any ministry? Did he show any fruit in his life which would honour God or deem him worthy of being called a disciple of Christ?

No! He spent his life stealing from people and didn't give God or anyone anything but contempt and yet this God, Who is love, turns to him and says, *"You're coming home to heaven with me brother."*

That encounter between Jesus and the thief on the cross was recorded and preserved by the Holy Spirit so that in every generation since that day, redeemed, enlightened children of God could be given the most powerful religion-busting tool in our possession in and through the most simple and life-changing story you can share when people ask you what the church is all about. That is what the church which Jesus birthed and promised to build is all about: unbridled grace, unconditional, incomprehensible love, undeserved, total forgiveness, complete redemption, restoration and reconciliation with our God for eternity.

Tragically, that's not what many man-made institutions called 'church' are about and that's why so many people have not yet been introduced to the Jesus Whom that thief encountered on his deathbed. They have been introduced to a counterfeit Jesus or no Jesus at all. How do I know that? It's simple really. Look at the shrinking church across our nation!

I can provide you with a truckload of research, studies, surveys and analysis from the experts as to why this is the case, particularly in the western world. I can then give you another two truckloads of books on evangelism and church growth containing every formula under the sun to grow the church. I am embarrassed to admit that I have actually wasted a lot of time wading through the contents of those books many years ago.

Then the scales fell from my eyes as I began to see what God sees. It is as simple as it is shocking! The mission of Christ, in and through the church, is so very, very simple and the only reason we have complicated it and have truckloads of solutions which don't work is because we refuse to accept just how simple it really is. We just need to meet and fall in love with the real Jesus again.

The Church needs to encounter the same Jesus that thief encountered on the cross. At that point, we will once again have the attention of the world in the most positive, life-changing way, because we will once again be rooted and established in love, not law; relationship, not religion; Jesus Christ, not a facsimile of Him which repels people, but the real Jesus Who always draws people to Himself.

It is that Jesus Who promised to build His Church and that's exactly what He's doing. As that happens, the world will no longer be talking about Royal Commissions, abuse and corruption within the Church, or the totally irrelevance of the Christian faith in our post-modern, post-Christian, 'enlightened' society. The world will once again be talking about these Christians who are known by their love, their acceptance, their grace and the power and presence of God in their lives.

Christ crucified, risen and reigning among us will be Christ glorified and <u>then</u> the promise of Christ to build His church against which even the gates of hell itself cannot prevail, will become a reality right before our eyes.

You and I get to be part of that revolution as we, and those to whom we minister and teach and encourage each day, become rooted and grounded in the life-changing, nation-transforming love of God.

I invite you to pray with me again …

> *Holy Spirit of God we ask again that You would show us our hearts. Reveal our foundation and show us if we have built our lives, our faith, our theology or 'our' church and its ministries on anything other than the bedrock of Your amazing grace and love in Christ.*

Show us if we have built our life on somebody else's good ideas. We may have built our life on the foundation of a parent's expectations. We may have built our life on the expectations of society or the Church or friends, rather than on the bedrock of Your love and grace.

Lord, show us our hearts today and give us the courage to let You re-establish us and renew our foundations, so that our 'house,' our life and then by extension, the life of the church, is built upon the rock of Your love and the simplicity and power of the gospel of Jesus Christ, in Whose name we pray and for Whose glory we live, Amen.

CHAPTER ELEVEN
Beautiful Love

What comes into your mind when I say the word: *beautiful?* Just think about it for a moment now. When I say the word *beautiful* - what picture or idea do you see or think about? Some will think of a sunset; some a mountain-top lookout; others will think of a special place they have visited in their travels. When thinking of beauty, sports fans might think of their sporting heroes at their prime and that last minute move from a sports star which won the game or that gold medal performance at an Olympic Games. Beauty for an architect may be a perfectly formed and functional building. Beauty for a poet might be a perfectly balanced couplet. Some people will use the word *beautiful* to describe a loved one or a very special friend. You may use the word in many other contexts.

We use the word *beautiful* all the time but you might be surprised to learn that Jesus only used it twice. Once in Matthew 23 in a more abstract comparative sense but then only once in a direct sense. There was one event in the life of Jesus that He judged to be of such supreme elegance, such aesthetic charm that He called it *beautiful*. This one event in His life was an act of love done to Him by an anonymous woman. Let's re-visit this story:

> *"Now the Passover and the Festival of Unleavened Bread were only two days away, and the chief priests and the teachers of the law were scheming to arrest Jesus secretly and kill him. "But not during the festival," they said, "or the people may riot."*

> *While he was in Bethany, reclining at the table in the home of Simon the Leper, a woman came with an alabaster jar of very expensive perfume, made of pure nard.*

She broke the jar and poured the perfume on his head. Some of those present were saying indignantly to one another, "Why this waste of perfume? It could have been sold for more than a year's wages and the money given to the poor." And they rebuked her harshly.

"Leave her alone," said Jesus. "Why are you bothering her? She has done a beautiful thing to me. The poor you will always have with you, and you can help them any time you want. But you will not always have me. She did what she could. She poured perfume on my body beforehand to prepare for my burial.

Truly I tell you, wherever the gospel is preached throughout the world, what she has done will also be told, in memory of her." (Mark 14:1-9)

Why did Jesus call this beautiful? What are the components of beauty in this scenario and are they repeatable by us? We began this journey together with me emphasising God's lavish, unconditional and eternal love for us and how we can experience that love. As we near the end now we will be talking about how we love God and others. There are many components to this act of love which Jesus called beautiful. But I want to explore four of them here.

1. *Beautiful love is risky*

This story has risk written all over it for this woman. To begin with, she crashes a party. That's risky. Secondly, she crashes a party and she is a woman! Given the status of women in this culture and time, this would have been risky in the extreme.

Then she does something guaranteed to be misunderstood and rejected by many. She breaks the perfume and pours it out, thereby bringing condemnation from those watching.

They thought she was crazy and the risk is then intensified because she doesn't know at this point whether Jesus will receive her affection or side with her critics. A further risk is obviously the cost involved. The text tells us that this perfume had the value of a year's wages. Can you imagine a $90,000 bottle of perfume being broken today and poured over someone's head?

If we want to participate in acts of love that can truly be called beautiful, the first thing we have to count on is that it will cost us some comfort. We will need to move out of our comfort zone; out of our area of control in order to perform those acts of love to Jesus and to His brothers and sisters in the church. We will be called upon to take risks and risking is very difficult for many of us.

I don't think that is because we are conservative by nature. You may think that's the way you were made but I believe you can tell a lot about our basic nature by simply observing children under the age of 5. Are they conservative in their expressions of love? No. They are lavish in love; they pour out affection and it's interesting that many of those who are restricted at that stage by Downe syndrome or some other intellectual impairment seem to hang on to that lavish, risky kind of love. They go on being open and free with their affection. They can maintain that child-like attitude to love while the rest of us 'mature' and get over it. We learn that there are certain people that you don't trust with your affection. We learn through bitter experience that we had better be careful about extending affection unilaterally - it's risky. We can get hurt and even be punished in the process.

So many of us (and I want the Holy Spirit to minister to you as you read this), many of us - deep down inside, associate love with pain. Well, today I believe the Lord wants to sever that connection.

There are many who will not take the risk again because they've been burnt before. I trust that the Lord will bring healing today which will allow us all to step out again.

Now what's the payoff for this woman? She loses $90,000 worth of perfume; she gets rebuked by the good people of the town; they criticise her for this vulnerable, risky act of love. So, what does she get out of it? Jesus defends her and declares to all of those present, and now to millions and millions of people down through history, that she has done a beautiful thing for Him - she has done what she could.

> "I tell you the truth, wherever the gospel is preached throughout the world, what she has done will also be told, in memory of her."

This pointless, senseless, risky, expensive act of love is now the means by which this woman and her act of love is made immortal. No act of love done for Jesus ever dies!

There are many things that Jesus did which aren't recorded. There are lots of things that the Apostles did which aren't recorded. This woman does one thing and it is repeated wherever this gospel is preached. What did she get for her risk? More than she ever dreamed of. She and her actions were made immortal. I put hundreds of hours every year into writing, preaching and recording.

If I keep that up for 20 more years, I guess there will be millions of my words out there in books and websites that will remain in circulation after I'm gone but it won't take long for all of that to vanish so that I am not even a memory to most. All that work, time and energy, will be forgotten. But everything that I did privately or publicly that was an act of love to Jesus is going to be remembered forever by Jesus! That's a pretty strong motivation to take a risk.

In the world of finance, the rule is usually low risk equals low potential payoff, high risk equals high potential payoff. If you want a guaranteed, government backed investment, the return will usually be comparatively low. However, there are growth funds in international markets which are returning so much more to investors - but there is a high risk attached. They could easily lose it all. High risk - high potential payoff; low risk - low potential payoff.

Maybe many of us have become too conservative in our love of Jesus and in our love of His people. The equation reads like this: If you want a real life you have to take some chances and step out of your comfort zone.

Now in finances you might decide that you don't want to risk your money. But imagine for a moment that you had an endless supply of cash. Imagine that you had a limitless credit line. Wouldn't you have a lot of fun investing in all kinds of things?

Wouldn't it be fun to take really big risks on investments knowing that if you lose it all there is more where that came from? Well, that's what you get if you're connected with God, and I'm not talking about money.

People hold their emotions and hold their love because they are afraid of investing it and seeing it wasted. But when you finally realise the truth of the Gospel which I have been preaching and writing till I drop for many decades now; when you realise that God's grace and love is an endless river flowing into your heart, flowing into your experience and that no matter how much you give to God and others, there is so much more where that came from; when you finally let that reality grip your heart and experience then you will have a wonderful time investing your love for the rest of your life!

That's the only reason I am still here. I have given my whole life to the Church Jesus birthed and promised to build and to the mission of Christ. I have continually emptied my soul before people; I have taken incredible risks in doing that; many have received what I've given with gladness, joy and appreciation. Some have rejected it, criticised it, abused it and thrown it back in my face. But that's OK.

I take the same risks with everyone - I have to. Some will pay off, some will not, but I keep going only because there is an endless river of love and grace and power flowing into me from God!

I long for the day, I would give anything to see the day when the church of Jesus Christ fully understands the grace and love of God and moves out of its comfort zone, stops 'playing church' and gets on with the job of really loving the world into the kingdom of God!

Everybody has this same potential – it's simply a matter of understanding it and acting on it and watching the revolution in your life.

The world is full of people who pull their heads in the moment they get hurt and never take risks again. Let me assure you, I know how it feels to be hurt that way; I know how it feels to have your good intentions and loving acts splattered all over your face; I know how hard it is to wash that stuff off - get a refill of God's unconditional love and move out again to face the next possible rejection.

But I also know what kind of life I would be living if I let that rejection stop me from taking any more risks.

The second principle that we see in this story in Mark 14, which makes this act of love beautiful is an important one:

2. Beautiful love seizes the moment

Timing is critical - for beautiful love. Jesus said: *the poor you have with you always* ... the pressure for timing is not there. *You had the poor with you yesterday - you'll have them tomorrow - they'll always be there ... but I won't. I am soon to be crucified. So take this opportunity now, take this risk ... go for it right now or you'll miss the boat. It will be too late.*

Beautiful love ceases the moment.

Jesus is on His way to be crucified, so this woman cannot wait. She cannot go home and pray about it. She cannot go home and diversify her investments to cover the loss of this perfume. She can't go home and pour half of it into another container to save some money. She has to risk everything right here and now and launch tonight.

> *"Leave her alone," Jesus said. "She's done something beautiful for me. You'll always have the poor, but she has responded in love to the here and now."*

How many times have you thought of showing affection to someone and the moment came and went and it was too late. How many times have you thought of a gift you'd like to send somebody but then you let the moment pass and for one reason or another the timing was off. How often have you thought of picking up the phone to call someone, only to discover that tomorrow was too late to do it? It's true, when it comes to beautiful love, the timing may be critical.

Sometimes missing an opportunity to love is not just a risk for the other people it's a risk for us as well. You've got to pay attention - when the moment to love comes, when the moment to risk comes, seize the moment! Beautiful love offers us windows of opportunity to cease the moment.

Let's be praying that God gives us the discernment to see the moment and seize the moment.

Thirdly, love that Jesus calls beautiful, in addition to being risky, in addition to being time sensitive it is also lavish!

3. *Beautiful love is lavish*

When Jesus was in Bethany, a women came in and poured out a jar of very expensive perfume on Him. She lavished it on him and people said: *"What waste! This could have been sold for a year's wages and given to the poor!"* The Bible says here that love is lavish and when I make the point of saying that love is lavish, I am not limiting that lavishness to the expense of money. I include the expense of emotion and time and energy. That is to say: love does whatever it has to do; love goes to whatever lengths it has to go to get the job done. This woman could not take a little drop of perfume and anoint Jesus in a symbolic way - she had to use it all.

In a risky way, seizing the moment, she gave what was needed to get the job done. By some kind of revelation she knew that Jesus was about to die. Jesus implies that. We don't know how she knew it - maybe she was the only person who believed Him when he said he must go up to Jerusalem to die. We don't have the details but we do know that she saw something that needed to be done and she poured herself and her treasure out to the fullest extent to get the job done - even though all of her counsellors said: this is a waste.

God really likes this lavish, apparently wasteful love. He really likes it. It brings joy to His heart. It's not that we go out looking for lost causes to pour ourselves into, it's that when He presents something to us to pour our lives into, we do it and we don't count the cost.

We may get no payoff at all - but by doing what God wants we have participated in life. We cannot calculate a return on our love for other people, but there is a big return. Do you know what you get if you 'waste' your love on one of God's creatures? You get Jesus saying to you when you finally meet Him face to face: *"Thank you doing this beautiful thing for me - for as much as you did it to the least of these my children - you did it to Me. Well done, good and faithful servant, well done."* Do you want to hear Jesus say that to you?

Love is risky, it seizes the moment, it's lavish - it goes to whatever extent it needs to in order to get the job done, but mystery of mysteries:

4. Beautiful love come best through brokenness

"While he was in Bethany, reclining at the table in the home of a man known as Simon the Leper, a woman came with an alabaster jar of very expensive perfume, made of pure nard. She broke the jar and poured the perfume on his head."

This perfume was very costly and very potent. It was used, not just for women to smell good. It was used to anoint honoured guests when they came to your home. It was kept in a large jar with this tiny little hole in the top. To use the perfume you would dip a slender little straw or dipstick into the hole and pull it out and then dab it on your most honoured guest. So, it was taken out one drop at a time. But this woman had a job to do. If she had turned it upside down, it wouldn't have come out. So, what did she do? She broke the vase!

Let me state the obvious here. The only way to get at this treasure is to break something and the only way to get the most beautiful and potent and costly love out of you and me is through our brokenness.

It is not ultimately in our strength that we do our best work. If you've been around long enough - you already know this. If you haven't then let me tell you that your best love, your best pastoral care does not some through your own skills in ministry. It does not come by having the right words to say at the right time - it comes through brokenness.

Our most costly treasures reach people through the cracks in our own hearts. That's just the nature of love. I do not fully understand it, but it is absolutely true. I can give you thousands of examples of this love but I guess the most profound is the one which stands at the centre of our faith: the supreme breaking; the supreme act of love; the supreme gift and that is the death of Jesus Christ over 2,000 years ago on the cross of Calvary.

The death of Jesus for us was a beautiful thing and it was risky. There was no guarantee that we would respond to His sacrifice. His act of love was incredibly risky. It also goes without saying that it was lavish. All of heaven was bankrupt - all the glories of heaven were emptied on the cross of Christ but the payoff is the salvation of the world, for God so loved the world that He gave His only Son. And all of this lavish, world-changing love came through what? Brokenness. It came through the breaking of a man on a criminal's cross.

How then shall you live in light of God's revelation today? Let me suggest how. Firstly, decide today that you will develop a lifestyle of risk; don't be conservative with your love. Because if you don't express it, you don't live and you deny the rest of us the life that you could give. So, take some risks with love. Risk feeling foolish; risk taking chances; risk being rebuked - knowing there's lots more where that came from. Any love that you give is poured back into you. Give and it will be given to you.

Secondly, pray for the discernment to spot the moment and then for the courage to seize the moment. This should be a daily prayer, for God provides those moments all the time. We just need to see them and embrace them.

Thirdly, plan on it being lavish and costly as you pour out your love. That's a given - it's guaranteed. So, plan ahead of time to be moved out of your comfort zone – sometimes a long way out.

Finally, never expect to do it in the power of your own personal strength but expect for your best work to come in and through your own weakness and brokenness.

Come, Holy Spirit. Empower us, teach us, transform us. Enable us to love as God loves. In Jesus' name, amen.

CHAPTER TWELVE
How to Love as Jesus Loves

We've spent a lot of time in this book thinking about God's love for us and that is really important. We've heard a lot about the various ways that we can respond to God's love; be more effectively touched, helped and transformed by God's love. We've been reminded of the need to be rooted and grounded in love and as individuals in the church we all need to grasp that. But we have also heard that love is incomplete and love will go sour in us if we do not learn and develop the skill to express that love to God and to other people. God effectively says to us all: *"If you want to love Me, love other people."*

Jesus will say on that final day: *"You fed Me, you clothed Me, you comforted Me, you visited Me in prison."* And we'll say: *"What? We never even saw you - let alone fed you, visited you, comforted you or clothed you."* Then He will say on that day: *"When you did it to the least of these, you did it to me."*

God makes it very clear to us: *"If you want to love Me, worship is fine - I delight in that; but if you really want to love me, start giving My love away to somebody else."* So now we are going to conclude this study by talking about the skill - the 'how to' of loving people and completing this interchange of love that God initiated in us through Jesus Christ, in which we have been trying to get rooted and grounded.

> *"Follow God's example, therefore, as dearly loved children and walk in the way of love, just as Christ loved us and gave himself up for us as a fragrant offering and sacrifice to God." (Ephesians 5:1-2)*

Paul is saying we are to love each other; we are to live a life of love; a life characterised by love.

God is love, so as Christians if we want to live in God we will live in love. More specifically, we are to live a life of love as Christ did. To put it another way, in Jesus own words: *"Love one another as I have loved you."*

Now that sounds daunting, doesn't it? Nobody really takes that seriously, do they? We don't really love people as Christ loved us. Surely His love is so far beyond any ability we have to comprehend it - let alone express His love in the same way.

The magnitude of Jesus' love seems way beyond us and so this whole discussion can seem too abstract. But everything we're exhorted to do in the New Testament - God expects us to do and also, by His Holy Spirit, He has empowered us to do it. God's bidding is God's enabling. That just means that He will give us the power to do what He asks us to do. That's why Paul said: *"I can do all things through Christ Who strengthens me."* (Philippians 4:13)

It is not from our native ability that we do this - we are made competent ministers by His Holy Spirit so we can do what God has commanded us to do and we are called to love each other as Christ loved us. So exactly how do we do that? Well, what I want to do in this chapter is try to bring this high and lofty expectation to love each other down into our real world. I hope I can achieve that in part as the Holy Spirit leads.

I want to suggest to you that when we think about how Christ loved us that we should not think about how 'big' He loved us - but specifically how He manifested that love. What did He actually do to love people? What were His skills? How did He make choices? How did He get His love to others? The 'how-to' is what I want to address in this chapter.

When you read the gospels, you will notice that Jesus loved people in a very free, creative and spontaneous way. He didn't love everybody the same way. He tailored His love to each person as an individual. For one person He spat on their face and healed them - an interesting expression of love, don't you think? To another He stood at a distance and wept; another He touched; to another He spoke; to another He scolded, in love.

His love was adapted to the individuals according to their needs. So, it was creative; it was sensitive to the person; it was situational; it was free - specifically free of rules. He loved in a non-religious, even anti-religious way.

In Jesus' day, a Pharisee was somebody who really knew the law, and really thought they were God's chosen and favourite and higher echelon believer. Well, if a Pharisee was asked how to love they would most likely think back to the Torah - the Law. For many it had become a system for living. You ask a question - they regurgitate Law No. 224 or Law No. 317 or whatever. They had over 600 rules for every situation and so much of the Rabbinic writing is defining what people should do in specific circumstances.

That's the way religion was then and that's the way religion operates now. It may be a little more sophisticated and the rules may be unwritten in some cases - but it's still the same.

This kind of legalistic lifestyle is easier to live in many ways. You don't have to use your imagination, you don't have to hear from the Holy Spirit, you don't have to take any risks. If you've got a rule or a law you just obey it and that's it.

But Jesus does the exact opposite. He breaks the Pharisee's rules in the pursuit of a life of love and He teaches us to do the same.

For instance, the law said you must love your neighbour and hate your enemies, but Jesus said: *"Ignore that rule and love your enemy too."* A rule said: if someone asks for your shirt, give it to them - Jesus said: *"Go way beyond that law - give them your coat too."* Jesus not only taught creative rule-breaking in loving people, He also practised creative rule-breaking in loving people. The Law taught: don't ever touch a leper - and if you do it accidentally, you are unclean for a period of time. Jesus didn't think much of that law - He not only touched lepers - He embraced them and went out of His way to do so. He broke the rules for the sake of love.

There were religious rules that should have prevented Jesus from associating with women the way He did. He ignored those rules too for the sake of love. The law said: don't heal on the Sabbath - what does Jesus do? He goes out of His way to heal on the Sabbath. The reason He did that was simple - He found some sick people who needed healing and that was more important than the day on the calendar and what the Pharisees had turned that into. If a law tells you to do something that violates somebody's real needs, then that is not a Godly interpretation of that law. But the Pharisees, who were strict adherents and custodians of the law - just couldn't get it. They protested loudly wherever Jesus went: *"The Law says don't heal on the Sabbath - you're healing on the Sabbath - that's wrong and that's all there is to it!"*

Now we have this problem, don't we? You may already be thinking there is a conflict here. I am happy to acknowledge that we do have a tension here. Jesus said quite clearly in Mark 5:17: *"I came into the world not to destroy the law but to complete it."* Well, what do you do with that in light of what I've just said about Jesus breaking the law every day? How do you reconcile Mark 5:17 with the way Jesus acted? He went against the rules, He defied the laws and we know that Jesus only did what He saw the Father doing.

Everything Jesus did was right and He was completely without sin. How can He then say that He did not come to destroy the law?

Well, let me give you the Apostle Paul's view:

> *"Let no debt remain outstanding, except the continuing debt to love one another, for whoever loves others has fulfilled the law. The commandments, "You shall not commit adultery," "You shall not murder," "You shall not steal," "You shall not covet," and whatever other command there may be, are summed up in this one command: "Love your neighbour as yourself." Love does no harm to a neighbour. Therefore, love is the fulfilment of the law." (Romans 13:8-10)*

> *"You who are trying to be justified by the law have been alienated from Christ; you have fallen away from grace. For through the Spirit we eagerly await by faith the righteousness for which we hope. For in Christ Jesus neither circumcision nor uncircumcision has any value. The only thing that counts is faith expressing itself through love." (Galatians 5:4-6)*

Therefore, there's something about living a life of love that completes the law - even though it may appear to supersede it or even run contrary to it. There is a higher law and it is the law of love. There is a completion to the practical, holy character and intent of the law and that is to love other people according to the power, wisdom and righteousness revealed to us in Christ, by the Holy Spirit.

Now again, the central question is: how then did Jesus love? What were the principles that guided Him? Without the railways tracks of religion to run on, like the Pharisees had, we seem to be cut adrift.

Someone reading this now might be thinking: *"Hey, I heard something about this in a philosophy course once, don't they call this situational ethics? Are we to look at everything situationally and so there is no real right or wrong and so we do everything according to the circumstances that present to us?"*

Absolutely not! That is certainly not what I am saying and not what Jesus did or the apostle Paul taught. This is much more creative and much more interesting and I get really excited about this because it's Biblical truth and it will take you on to maturity in Christ. But I have to say that there is very little market for it in the body of Christ. There is such a small market for creative, spontaneous, real Christianity.

For the most part, people are so much happier if you just tell them what to do - no questions asked. Then they don't have to think; they don't have to hear from the Holy Spirit. Just give them some rules and regulations and although that is spiritual abuse and manipulation - a lot of people seem to prefer it to real freedom and maturity in Christ.

But I'm going to take the risk anyway, without rules, without laws, without having something to hide behind to give us an excuse for what we do, to give us a chapter and verse or rule No. 224 justification for our actions.

When you take that all away, are we then cut adrift? Are we on our own? Do we just make ad-hoc choices? The answer is no. Absolutely not. There is something far, far better than proof-texting as a way to live your life and it's Godly, it's holy and it's the way Jesus lived Himself as a man when He walked among us.

Jesus knew how to love, He knew how to creatively surpass the laws that He was given by His tradition. He knew how to do that and here are some reasons.

He was rooted and grounded in His Father's love.

When He dealt with people Jesus never tried to manipulate them, use them or abuse them. He didn't need to. He was going to look out for their best interests because He had already been taken care of by His Father. He was secure in His Father's love – He didn't need the affirmation of others and so His motive was always love.

He had discernment.

He knew Scripture and He was filled with the Holy Spirit so He could see what the Father was doing and He followed suit. When the Father wanted to heal on the Sabbath - even though it went against the Pharisee's rules - Jesus healed on the Sabbath, because He had the discernment to know that is what His Father was doing that day. It's that simple.

He related to people.

He had some close friends who could speak into His life. We have examples of Peter and other people exhorting Jesus. He had cultivated a relationship with a few people that was strong enough for them to feel free to question His actions. This is God we are talking about. He was always right. But even though He was always right, He created an atmosphere around Him where people felt the freedom to speak their mind. He was always open to people - He was in relationship with them. They were valued and affirmed.

He did everything out in the open.

He did it in the light. If you follow these four principles - you can love God and do anything you like – because if you genuinely love God, you will always do what you see the Father doing. You will always please God. This is how Jesus loved creatively, which sometimes followed the Pharisee's law to the letter and at other times he violated their rules.

You know it is as true today as it was in Jesus' day - many people in the church consciously or subconsciously try to find rules to govern their faith so they can feel secure and I can understand why they do that. If you are riding in a railway carriage you can relax and even go to sleep and pay little or no attention to where you are going. As long as you stay on the tracks laid before you, you're safe.

Whereas in a car - it's a whole different story. There is a road - but there are no tracks so you have to actually pay attention; look ahead; make decisions and be responsible. All analogies break down at some point - but I guess that one explains to me, at least, the difference between the way the Pharisees lived and the way Jesus lived and calls us to live.

Now if you follow those principles you can love God and do as you please! These are no rules. There are guiding principles; there are observations of fact in Jesus' life and in the lives of those who follow His example. If you're one of them, then you will live a life of creative, Spirit-led free love which will be the highest expression of love that humans can give each other.

Now let me be really honest at this point and say that it is quite possible that for many people this will all fall on deaf ears. I don't say that with anyone in mind; I don't say that in an accusing or judgmental manner. I say it as a statement of historical fact. It's part of our fallen nature to want to fall back on the rules and criticise others according to the rules.

The fact is this: the call to spiritual maturity is a call to do what Paul tells us: *"To love people as Christ loved us,"* and Christ loved us first of all by ensuring that He Himself was rooted and established in the Father's love; He remained close to and in tune with the Holy Spirit always;

He exercised discernment and did only what He saw the Father doing; He was always open to people; He had close relationships where people could speak into His life and He did everything out in the open, not allowing Satan, who lurks in the shadows, to gain a foothold.

It is my prayer that the Holy Spirit will use what I've shared in this chapter to bring you to a fuller understanding what it really means to love as Christ loved. It is my prayer that the Holy Spirit will use all that I have shared in this book to re-connect you to the priority of love in your relationship with God and with others.

I would encourage you to revisit this teaching and work your way through this book again in the future, perhaps with a highlighter in your hand as you take note of those things God wants to teach you and affirm in you. Spaced repetition is the best way to learn anything and so coming back to this again will be really helpful.

May God continue to draw us all closer to Himself and to each other as we more fully embrace the mission of Christ and our primary purpose in life – to love and be loved.